Dior

CHRISTIAN DIOR 1905–1957

FRANÇOISE GIROUD

Photographs
SACHA VAN DORSSEN

Project co-ordinator and Picture research
ANNE BONY

RIZZOLI
NEW YORK

First published in the United States of America in 1987 by
RIZZOLI INTERNATIONAL PUBLICATIONS, INC.
597 Fifth Avenue, New York, NY 10017

Copyright © 1987 A.D.A.G.P. and Editions du Regard,
14 rue de Mail, Paris 75002, Paris

English translation copyright
© 1987 Thames and Hudson Ltd, London

ISBN 0-8478-0860-2
LC 87-80880

Translated from the French by Stewart Spencer

Printed and bound in Spain

CONTENTS

Christian Dior at forty-five. When he looked at women, it was not to undress, but to dress them.
Photo by Irving Penn.

On the balcony in the Avenue Montaigne. The House of Dior extended
over five buildings, his empire over five continents.

It was the twelfth of February 1947.

The people of Paris were shivering with cold as the temperature fell to thirteen degrees of frost. Coal was in short supply, and the newspapers were out on an indefinite strike.

And so it came about that the French were the last to learn of a momentous event that had just taken place in a private mansion in the Avenue Montaigne: the event in question was the birth of a couturier. More than that, it was the birth of a fashion – perhaps even the birth of Fashion itself – a fashion which from that day forward was to be word of law from South America to the Australian subcontinent.

In a pearl-grey room a middle-aged man stood besieged by a throng of people, his chubby features scarred by lipstick, while an exceedingly ugly American lady, Carmel Snow, editor-in-chief of *Harper's Bazaar*, was heard to proclaim the historic words, 'It's quite a revolution, dear Christian. Your dresses have such a new look. They are wonderful, you know!'

New Look, the first collection to bear the name of Christian Dior, was thus baptized. It was an expression that was to catch on in every one of the world's countless languages.

Most of the American buyers had already left Paris, having bought all they wanted from Jacques Fath, Lelong, Piguet, Rochas, Balmain and Balenciaga. . . 'The poor things,' Carmel Snow remarked with her usual discernment. 'They'll have to come back.' And come back they did. So began a venture that was as brief as it was brilliant, a venture without equal in the whole history of fashion. There were other stars in the firmament, but Dior's star shone brightest.

From right to left, Carmel Snow, editor-in-chief of *Harper's Bazaar*, the photographer Richard Avedon, and Marie-Louise Bousquet. The eyes of America.

The day of the opening in February 1947. Rita Hayworth in the centre, the Begum Agha Khan to her right. A dazzling venture was about to begin. . . *Photos by Maywald.*

From the day when his name – spelt Diaure or d'Yorre – was first carried on agency wires, to the date of his sudden death, ten years later, at the age of fifty-two, his fame increased to the point where he was named alongside Stalin and Gandhi as one of the five best-known people in the world.

Letters reached him in their thousands, showering him with lavish praise, appeals for help, and abusive insults. 'You and your so-called genius have succeeded in disfiguring my wife. What would you say if I sent her to you now?' an enraged farmer wrote to him from Idaho. And an engineer from Texas warned him, 'Set foot in this State and I'll kick you out.'

Covering five continents, the Dior Empire was the first commercial empire to be founded entirely on fabric. The parent company in Paris that had begun with three ateliers soon numbered twenty-eight, employing 1400 men and women and extending over five whole buildings. Twenty-five thousand customers passed through Dior's salons each season, while distinguished visitors came to pay their respects as though at Napoleon's Tomb.

Dior was by no means the only couturier in Paris throughout these ten years, and he knew it. The proud genius of Cristobal Balenciaga cast a perpetual shadow over him at a time when Dior would have dearly loved to have reigned supreme. It was l'Autre who reigned supreme. But at Balenciaga's, mass was said for only a handful of votaries initiated into the cult of implacable elegance.

When the New Look exploded on to the scene, Dior suddenly found himself in a totally different world.

What was this New Look that brought him his meteoric rise to fame and which maintained his renown to the end? First and foremost it was a reaction against the fashion of the 1940s, which had been a time of shortages and want: narrow, short skirts, wide shoulders, voluminous hats, feet weighed down by platform soles. Then came inspiration. A spectacular lowering of the hemline was the most immediately obvious sign of the New Look, but it also transformed all the proportions of the female figure, restoring to it the most graceful contours of its natural form. A moulded bust issuing from a narrow waist, accentuated breasts, rounded hips beneath petticoat-length skirts, slender shoulders, hidden calves, and a neat little head: fashion, according to Dior, should bring back a sense of femininity by means of gentle curves. All the real and imaginary elegance of an engulfed past followed in its train.

An evening dress in its early stages. The quality of the stitching was all-important for Dior. *Photo by Bellini.*

Pearl-grey satin for an asymmetrical evening dress. The Winged Line.
1948. *Photo by Maywald.*

Dainty hands at work. Dior's seamstresses still knew the secrets of a
'labour of love'.

Delicate dresses, attractive and flattering, with that profusion of fabric that marked the end of wartime rationing – 'Diorama', the centre-piece of the winter collection, was forty metres in circumference – it was exactly what post-war women wanted. They did not know it, of course; Dior revealed it to them. Every fashion dies from disenchantment and is born of desire, crystallizing all that shimmers upon the surface of a society. The New Look, appearing from nowhere at a time when the war was still so tangibly close, coincided exactly with a violent desire that had still to find coherent expression. And so it was that a minor event in Paris, the creation of a new line, became an event on a world scale and, in the United States, something of a scandal. What? How dare this Frenchman hold patriotism in such utter contempt as to squander material? And what right did he have to conceal the legs of American ladies? Factions sprang up. People marched through the streets to the cries of 'Burn Christian Dior' and 'Christian Dior go home!'

Left of picture, Carmel Snow, the American whose historic words gave the New Look its name, and, to the right, Louise Dahl-Wolfe; Marcel Achard can be seen behind them. *Photo by Maywald.*

Christian Dior with Princess Margaret.
Photo by Maywald.

When Dior disembarked in New York on his way to Dallas, where he was to receive a fashion award, he was surprised to be asked by the official who examined his passport, 'Ah, you're the designer. . . What's all this about the skirt length?' Startled by the question, Dior swore that his skirts were not as long as all that. Fortunately he spoke English well. Reporters were waiting for him. To their amazement they saw only a very ordinary-looking man.

'He looks like no one in particular!' the man from the *New York Times* was heard to exclaim in his disappointment.

The fact is that, to look at, Christian Dior was by no means remarkable. On the contrary. He was a decent-looking individual, dressed by a good tailor, and betraying a stoutness which tended to overwhelm his other features; and that was all. Beneath the fine surface that covers those who are born with a silver spoon in their mouths, he bore no outward sign of the artist, resembling rather those donors who appear in paintings by the French School. He certainly did not conform to the common image of a homosexual designer.

In his boneless face, only the brown of his eyes commanded attention. When he looked at a woman, it was not to undress, but to dress her. That at least was the feeling they had when under his gaze.

Conservative to the point of seeming reactionary, and sensitive to all change, which he loathed, he had a preference for walled gardens, enclosed beds, maternal women: everything that gave him a sense of protection. Utterly French in his sophistication and in his taste for moderation, he detested exoticism, at least in the realm of fashion.

Such was his loathing of slovenly dress and behaviour, he would refuse to receive a visitor who was not wearing a tie; he had an equal disdain for familiarity, from which he sought to protect himself by dint of extreme civility. He loved good music, good food, meeting friends and playing parlour games, but nothing too complicated. His manner, moreover, was simple and cheerful. But he could be hard-hearted. He gave the appearance of being restrained and consciously civilized. A certain inner violence would sometimes be vented in outbursts of fury, those terrible outbursts of anger from which those who are gentle by nature may suffer; but such fits of temper were rare. When examined closely his face was seen to be that of a kind and sensitive man, a vulnerable individual in a permanent state of insecurity. He bore no outward trace of managerial calibre, no sign that he was the heir to five generations of Norman industrialists. Not only did he give every appearance of being the banal representative of bourgeois provincialism, he failed to radiate the least charisma or exude any personal magnetism. A curious phenomenon in view of the man's inner wealth.

Scarcely had he landed in New York when he found himself facing the American press, who accused him, with all the virulence of which American journalists are capable, of hiding women's legs. To his own surprise, the normally slow and taciturn designer discovered that in so formidable an exercise as a press conference – conducted, moreover, in English – he could none the less shine.

Humphrey Bogart and Lauren Bacall. A whole ceremonial was brought into play. . . *Photo by Maywald.*

Opposite: The New Look worn by Marlene Dietrich, seen here with her daughter. Black wool crêpe dress over a satin underskirt. *Photo by Horst.*

America was very soon conquered, and for many years accounted for 60 per cent of the company's turnover.

In Paris, where any woman at all adept with her hands could run up a *Corolle* skirt for herself, the women customers who flocked to the Avenue Montaigne were soon to discover that a dress by Dior was a little less simple than that.

Drawing on the oldest of French traditions, that of local handicrafts, and the 'labour of love', of which Dior's workforce still knew the secret, he brought into being a new conception of *haute couture*. Each of his dresses, lined throughout, was like a piece of architecture that rested upon its foundations. Darts were forbidden, especially bustline darts; a hot iron was used instead. 'A well-cut dress is one with few cuts,' Dior used to say. A sophisticated long-line brassière or *bustier* was made as part of the dress, and lined with two pieces of tulle placed in opposite directions to one another, a technique invented by the famous Madame Marguerite, the leading head seamstress of her day. Two fittings were necessary as a general rule, sometimes as many as three. At the final stage the astute eye of the technical director Madame Linzeler would ensure that the style and quality of the original model had been respected throughout.

Every article to emerge from the Dior ateliers was a work of art on which two hundred hours of labour were lavished, for the most part by hand, for in each of Dior's workshops there were only three sewing machines to be shared among forty women. Well-stitched garments, Dior would say, were those that fitted as snugly as a glove.

The indescribable pleasure of wearing a 'well-stitched' dress that was made to measure was denied to all but a very few; but imitation Dior, off-the-peg Dior, counterfeit Dior, sub-Dior and quasi-Dior, and all that Dior had inspired – these offered women a new way of seeing themselves, a view they adopted with a kind of fury.

The staircase on the occasion of another opening. Jean Cocteau and
Francine Weisweiller in the foreground, Serge Heftler-Loriche
to the right. *Photo by Maywald.*

In his private mansion in Passy. Luxurious softness, quilted upholstery, silks and wall-hangings. *Photo by Cecil Beaton.*

Dior at work on a sketch. The hands of the master. *Photo by Maywald.*

It goes without saying that Dior himself had no idea what he might be unleashing when he designed the ninety dresses that made up his first collection.

He was utterly lacking in vanity, claiming that his only desire was to become 'a good tailor'. 'To dress a handful of elegant women from polite society' – it was on this basis that he reached an agreement with his partner Marcel Boussac, though not without setbacks on the way.

Boussac was then at the height of his power and owned, among other more substantial assets, a fashion house that was famous in its day as 'Philippe et Gaston', which was now known simply as 'Gaston', and whose fortunes he wished to revive by enlisting the help of a designer.

'Gaston's' managing director was a childhood friend of Dior's; they had played together on the beach at Granville. The two men met by chance one day in the street. The first asked the second, 'Do you know of anyone capable of taking it on?' No, Dior could think of no one.

A second encounter followed the first, and again Dior confessed to feeling perplexed.

Not until the third such meeting, which again took place on the pavement that leads from the Rue Saint Florentin to the Rue Royale where he lived, did Dior suggest his own name. He was then working for Lucien Lelong and happy in his congenial surroundings. But Lelong's other designer, Pierre Balmain, had recently left to set up his own business, a move which had given Dior a slight sense of shock. 'What about me?' he had thought. 'Have I no ambition myself?' He was not too old at forty-one, but it was none too soon to act.

He paid a call on 'Gaston', but returned, discouraged, to Marcel Boussac, bearing with him a negative answer.

It was then that this timorous man all at once found the courage to divulge a plan that had come to obsess him – a plan to create his very own fashion house, small and exclusive, but operating within the best traditions of *haute couture* for the benefit of genuinely elegant women. All that would be produced there were dresses that appeared to be simple but which in reality were highly elaborate, dresses able to meet the demands of those foreign markets which the post-war boom was about to revive and which would turn to Paris for something new.

Boussac listened. A few days later his right-hand man, Henri Fayolle, was engaged in discussions with Christian Dior.

One of the last dresses designed by Dior for Lucien Lelong, black wool crêpe and black-and-white striped bayadère. 1946. *Photo by Chevalier.*

But suddenly Dior took fright, aghast at the thought of leaving Lelong and afraid, perhaps, of what he had started. Did he suspect Boussac of being no more than a common dealer in cotton? At all events, he broke off negotiations by telegram, and hurried to see his favourite clairvoyante, Madame Delahaye. Fortunately for Dior she was a clear-sighted woman who ordered him to renew his links with Boussac. 'All that may be offered to you later,' she told him, 'is as nothing compared to the chance that you have here today.'

Christian Dior and his favourite clairvoyante, Madame Delahaye.
Photo by Maywald.

Dior was not the man to doubt a clairvoyante's word. There was nothing he did not construe as a sign from beyond, as the voice of a destiny which he interpreted on the strength of superstitions that were both traditional and private. In this way he had made up his mind that his lucky number was 8, and that the letter M, the colour red, the stars, and the lily of the valley were all a source of good luck for him. His faith in such things was unfailing.

Negotiations with Boussac were therefore resumed, and the two soon reached an agreement. A second clairvoyante, consulted by a third party as to the fate of the projected fashion house, went into a trance and declared that 'This house will revolutionize fashion!'

'This confirmation of one clairvoyante by another finally gave me the strength to act,' Dior wrote in all seriousness.

It now became necessary to break the news to Lelong. Had the latter been less authoritarian, he might never have lost either Dior or Balmain, both of whom got on well together. But his vision was limited to whatever his customers wanted to find, and thus he denied his designers freedom of expression. He suggested that Dior might consider a partnership. But it was too late for that. The die had been cast. Dior agreed to design two further collections, the better to ensure a smooth transition to a new designer, and he undertook to supervise their manufacture. Always one to do things properly, Boussac had decided to invest some fifty million francs in the operation.

Dior a few days before the opening of his fashion house. He wanted to be 'a good tailor, one who would dress a handful of elegant women from polite society'.

The Grande Boutique, a heavy investment, in 1955. *Photo by Maywald.*

The sick-bay.

The dining hall.

The store-room. Dior was loved by all his staff, high or low, because he had time for them all. *Photo by Maywald.*

The hat room. It was by designing hats that Dior had sold his very first sketches at twenty francs each.

An atelier. Each garment that left the atelier was a work of art on which two hundred hours of labour had been lavished. *Photo by Bellini.*

One of the twenty-eight ateliers. In each atelier there were only three sewing machines among forty seamstresses.

New Look accessories: tambourin hat, calf-length petticoat, elbow-length gloves, curved belt. . . 1948. *Photo by Franck Scherschel – Life.*

As a designer, among other things, of 'petites gravures' (as fashion sketches are known in the trade), Dior had found himself working in fashion without having been destined for such a career. Unlike the majority of fashion designers, he had neither felt any precocious calling nor run up dresses for his sisters' dolls. His mother's elegance and sophistication, and the trappings of luxury with which she surrounded herself, had left him imbued with a vision of women to which he remained loyal to the end. But he scarcely knew how to hold a pencil; only enough to reproduce the curve of an arching leg in a high-heeled shoe, an image that recurs with obstinate frequency in the books he used at school.

Above all else, his father's fortune – the wealth of a well-to-do bourgeois – was of a kind to spare him from having to earn his own living. His family hailed from the Channel resort of Granville, where they owned a number of factories, producing fertilizers and chemical products, which had been founded by Dior's great-great-grandfather in 1832. They led a life of well-established comfort. Granville, a fashionable resort in its day and the family fief, so to speak, was Christian's birthplace, and a town to which he remained fondly attached for the rest of his life. He spent his earliest childhood there in a vast pink and grey house jutting out over the Channel. A small, well-behaved boy under the care of a German governess, he retained a delightful memory of the walled-in garden and of the 'gentle and leisurely provincial life' from which he felt himself 'wrenched' when his parents decided to move to Paris. Even then he abhorred all change.

By the age of eighteen he had become an artistically gifted young man – as is said of those people whose gifts lie in no one direction. Tempted by architecture, he toyed with the notion of enrolling at Art School, but his parents opposed the idea. Enamoured of music, he obtained their permission to follow a course in composition, and developed a passion for the works of Les Six, and then for the so-called

Ecole d'Arcueil, while, as an obedient son, he pretended to study political science. It was during this period that he composed the ballet *Treize danses,* a piece that was later performed in the 1940s. But it was as a lover of painting that, at the age of twenty-two, he decided to open a gallery.

He described himself at this time in the following words: 'It was a question of running as fast as possible in order not to miss a single preview or party, but rather to enjoy the unique privilege of being at one with the century in committing the follies of youth. The privilege of dancing at all hours, whatever the cost, of staying awake all night, of listening to negro music, of carefree awakenings, or drunken revels devoid of nausea, of light-hearted love affairs and serious friendships; but above all else it was the privilege of "being available". . . We were as "available" then as people are "otherwise engaged" today. I took advantage of this watchword to explore the whole of Paris, a Paris that was new and inventive, cosmopolitan and intelligent, and prodigal of all that was genuinely new. I spent much of my time with art dealers. Modern art still had an air of black mass about it. But black was in vogue at that time.'

Resigned to the natural bent of so eccentric a son, his parents gave him the sum of capital that he needed to set up his own gallery, but on one condition: that his name should not figure in the corporate name. To see 'Dior' on the front of a shop was more than his parents could ever have borne.

The next three or four years were a time of great happiness for Christian Dior and his friend and partner, Jean Bonjean. The gallery they owned – at the end of a cul-de-sac in the Rue de la Boétie – did a thriving trade. Max Jacob and Jean Cocteau were the mainstays of its support, together with Henri Sauguet, Pierre Gaxotte and Christian Bérard, a joyful band of men. Collectors rallied round Dior when misfortune struck his family. His elder brother Raymond succumbed to an incurable illness; their exquisite mother died of grief; and then there were the endless consequences of the stock exchange crash of 1929 and of unfortunate property investments in Neuilly, with the result that the family found itself ruined in a matter of days.

When he was fourteen years old, the young Dior had had his palm read at a fair in Granville, and the palmist had told him, 'You'll find yourself penniless, but women will always bring you good luck, and it is through them that you'll be successful. You will profit greatly from women, and be obliged to make many sea-crossings.'

The first part of the prediction had now come true. Dior was without a *sou* to his name. Strange to relate, this was the very moment that he chose to set off for the Soviet Union with a group of architect friends. In a fit of youthful indignation, he had called his father a 'filthy bourgeois'. He appears to have thought that the crisis then threatening the Western world could be solved if the solution were sought elsewhere. But his journey had all the appearance of escapism, and it turned him for ever away from a system so little made for a man like Dior.

He returned from the Soviet Union to find his partner financially ruined like so many others, his family retired to Granville where they led a life of seclusion, his rooms in the Rue Albéric Magnard abandoned, and his cosy world destroyed for ever.

The young Dior, so cultured and cultivated, so delicate and so sensitive to all manifestations of art and beauty, the youth who had been shielded by his parents from the realities of life was now to learn what life was really about. And that was a subject on which he had had no instruction. His past life had slipped from his grasp, and only his friends remained. One after another they gave him shelter, unaware that when he came home in the evening it was without having eaten. He sold off the paintings that remained from his gallery at deplorable personal cost, left his associate and joined Pierre Colle, who managed a shop in the Rue Cambacérès where the Surrealists exhibited their work.

It was at Pierre Colle's that Salvador Dali held his first exhibition. But now was not the time to sell paintings, good, bad or indifferent. Incapable of finding his way out of the tunnel in which he saw himself, Dior went through months of distress, the mere recollection of which was a source of great pain to him, and scarcely improved by the memory of several wild parties. A small group of young men of Dior's own age who shared the same tastes and the same destitution had a certain fondness for celebration: a masked ball would be held at one of their houses, charades at another (a game that Dior adored), or else they would dine out at the Boeuf sur le Toit where Moyses, the owner, generously fed his old friends free of charge now they were down on their luck.

The problem of where to live continued to obsess them. Some of the group encountered magnanimous hotel-keepers; Dior, a high-class tramp, found refuge in a building that was being demolished. But the roof leaked and he came home one day to find neither water nor electricity in his garret.

Only illness was needed to complete this sad little picture, and sure enough, he soon fell ill. And a serious illness it proved to be. His friends clubbed together to pay for a trip to the mountains.

He returned a year later, fully recovered, having spent the months of enforced rest doing tapestrywork. But it was now a question of seeking offers of work; his bohemian life was over. Insurance companies, banks and accountancy vacancies – he read the small ads, queued up with the other applicants, submitted copies of his curriculum vitae, and a hundred times over was turned down as unsuitable – including a job at Lelong's where he applied for an administrative post. And then. . . then his luck changed.

All that remained of his earlier ruin was a canvas by Dufy, a *Plan of Paris* commissioned by Poiret to decorate one of his barges from days of former glories. Having lost all his money, Poiret had sold the canvas to Dior, who in turn had had the good fortune to resell it at a not unfavourable price. And since he had clearly emerged from the wood, a designer friend Jean Ozenne (who was later to pursue a career as an actor) offered to share his apartment with Dior.

Ozenne was held in regard by the designers and agents to whom he sold his fashion sketches. Seeing him at work, Dior idly began to imitate him. As a start he traced models in magazines. Ozenne encouraged him, and a friend of his, the American designer Max Kenna, taught him how to hold a brush and how to use colour. It was a happy Ozenne who returned home one evening having sold six of Dior's designs at twenty francs each.

It was the first money that Dior had ever earned with his very own hands, and he never forgot the exhilaration that it gave him. Who, indeed, could forget such a feeling? He was thirty years old. Destiny had led him along a strangely circuitous route before introducing him to the role for which he was best fitted; but he was finally saved. All that he needed now was to serve an apprenticeship in his new profession.

The first sketches that he made for dresses were unsatisfactory and badly received, but the designs that he made for hats found buyers. He persisted and worked hard. Two friendly critics, Michel de Brunhoff, the head of *Vogue,* and the interior designer Georges Geffroy guided his early, tentative steps. He was soon to be seen outside fashion warehouses, waiting to sell his designs one by one. *Le Figaro* asked for some sketches for its women's pages, and he applied himself to the task. The star of Robert Piguet was in the ascendant when Geffroy introduced him to Dior. Piguet bought some designs from him, and then asked him to create some models for his mid-season collection. Dior designed four, and Piguet allowed him to watch while they were being made. He was taken on as a designer in 1938, and from then on felt sheltered from all future risks. 'Café anglais', a hound's-tooth dress over a linen petticoat, was the success of the season. Christian Bérard searched high and low in an attempt to find out who the lucky designer had been. 'It was then that I knew I'd arrived,' said Dior.

Piguet was not one of the major couturiers. His actual technique of dressmaking was really quite basic, but he knew that elegance lay solely in simplicity, and Dior learned a valuable lesson from him: the art of reduction.

When recalling this period in the history of fashion, the normally charming and affable, courteous and kind-hearted Dior would lose his temper when speaking of Schiaparelli, who at that time held sway, embodying all that Dior most detested – uproar and noise, provocative actions, and the translation of Surrealist art into the language of fashion. Alone among the great names, that of 'Schiap' was capable of provoking acerbic remarks on Dior's lips.

In Dior's view the great designers of the inter-war years had been Molyneux, with his small harsh dresses, and the imperial figure of Coco Chanel – Chanel whom, together with Madeleine Vionnet, he regarded as the founder of modern fashion, but whose personality he found over-powering. He retained the dazzling memory of a society ball at which Coco Chanel and Misia Sert had both appeared in dresses of lace, a very picture of elegance. There were all manner of balls in Paris in 1939, common practice for those who are living on the edge of a volcano. Dior was there with the rest of them. He was a man in love. For Piguet he designed a daring collection – 'amphora' dresses which restored to women their rounded hips. But his time had not yet come; the Army demanded his presence, and not to make trenchcoats either. The anti-militarist designer professed to an anarchist outlook that was then in vogue in the circles which he frequented, and refused to train for an officer squad. It was thus as a private sapper that Dior landed at Mehun-

With Robert Piguet. A certain little hound's-tooth dress over a broderie
anglaise petticoat. . . *Photo by Maywald.*

sur-Yèvre, in the region of Berry, where he spent a year wearing clogs and where he made a disturbing discovery: he liked the land. It was here all around him, and he felt at his ease, far away from all that had hitherto made up his world. The white-handed aesthete devoted himself to the slow and difficult work that went on in the fields, enthralled by the seasonal cycle and the mysteries of germination. Was he of peasant stock? In going back through the generations every Frenchman finds soil on his shoes. But until that moment nothing had seemed so strange to Dior as Nature herself in the wondrous mystery of her workings. The revelation it gave him was to mark him for life and to affect his choice of residence when the time came.

At the Moulin du Coudret at Milly, where he engaged the services of a colourful Polish gardener called Ivan, visitors would find themselves walking on a carpet of flowers. Dior was a memorable sight in his sewer-worker's boots, deliberating, with all the seriousness of a man who knows what he is doing, as to the best position for planting a willow; only with raspberry-bushes was he at a loss.

At the Colle Noire, his property in the Var where he hoped to end his days, you could walk among vines and jasmine.

He claimed that he felt reassured when close to the soil. But the source of his lack of assurance was something he never explained, though obliged, of necessity, to speak a good deal of himself. No doubt not even Dior himself knew what childhood terrors had taught him to feel so guilty, and hence so threatened. On the day that his first collection was revealed to the world in February 1947, he was heard to mutter the words, 'What have I done? What on earth have I done?' Even at the height of his fame, he was still a prey to anxiety, surprised by his own audacity as though by the act of some spiteful, intractable *doppelgänger*.

The experience he gleaned from the land in 1939/40 allowed him to survive the débâcle. Upon being demobilized he was given the sum of

800 francs, and with it he travelled to Caillan, a village in the Var where his father and sister Catherine – later to be deported – had taken refuge. Once again the family was left unprovided for. All they had to their name was a mere strip of land.

Helped by his sister, Dior pulled up the flowers, dug over the soil, and planted vegetables. They eked out a living by growing peas and green beans, and by going on foot to the markets in Cannes and the neighbouring villages, where they sold their produce in person. As if by miracle, a cheque for a thousand dollars arrived from America, sent by a friend in exchange for the last few paintings from Dior's now defunct gallery, and enabling the family to hold out until their first harvest.

By the time Piguet had succeeded in renewing contact with his erstwhile designer, in the hope of encouraging his return to Paris, Dior had become a farmer, living according to the rhythm of the sun, using candles to light his home, and feeling a certain sense of well-being, however harsh the days may have been. Once again Dior hesitated, so that when, at the end of 1941, he turned up at Piguet's, his place was already taken. At a loss as to what to do next, he confided his troubles in Paul Caldaguès, who introduced him to Lucien Lelong. Lelong took him on straightaway. Not everyone was unhappy in Paris under the Occupation, and the fashion houses could scarcely be said to have been short of customers – far from it, indeed, though finding textile suppliers must have cost the designers a headache or two.

Six years later Dior was still with Lelong, having appreciably increased his practical knowledge of dressmaking skills in the meantime, and having come to terms with his own demands. Through his contact with leading head seamstresses, he learned the importance of what, for him, was the essential principle of dress design, namely a feeling for the grain of a fabric – for any dress to be a success, one must know how to handle the natural movement of the material.

Dior was thus master of his *métier* when he entered the arena alone. Having dreamt of building in stone, he had become an architect in the ephemeral world of fashion. And it is this highly elaborate 'architecture' which is Dior's personal trademark.

It remains, however, a fact that no amount of skill would have made him the reigning monarch of fashion had it not been for the seismic shock waves set off by the New Look and the sensible commercial strategy used to prolong them.

Dior was no business man. His personal dealings with money were simple enough: he spent it. As soon as his fashion house was successfully established, he began to live like a lord. He bought and converted the Moulin du Coudret at Milly. The river was tamed, marshland reclaimed, the forest cut back, and buildings restored to turn them into a pleasant place to live; the walls were covered in chintz and an unfinished tapestry invited passing guests to add a stitch towards its completion.

He left the Rue Royale with its four flights of stairs, and installed himself in a place more suited to his new situation, a small private house in the Boulevard Jules Sandeau, a hundred yards from the rooms in which he had lived as a youth. The task of decorating the house was entrusted to Victor Grandpierre, Georges Geffroy and Pierre Delbée.

Its Louis XIV setting revealed to his friends what he wanted most – luxurious softness, quilted upholstery, silks and wall-hangings, canopied beds – he was unable to sleep unless his bed was enclosed by thick curtains – silver taps, custom-made door handles, and a winter garden like the one at Granville, a disparate assemblage of sensuous objects and pieces of furniture that had but a single quality in common – they were all of the very best quality. Dior bought a good deal, and he paid a good deal, but all that he bought was good.

A Spanish butler of the old school dressed him each morning as though he were Louis XIV. And a *chef de cuisine* concocted delicious

Le Moulin du Coudret at Milly-la-Forêt. Dior's first house.
Photo by Maywald.

The summer dining-room at the Moulin.

One of the rooms at the Moulin: there were always curtains to protect him
at night. *Photos by Maywald.*

A dressing-table in one of the rooms at the Moulin. *Photo by Maywald.*

desserts that helped to maintain the paunch which gave him some cause for concern, though his love of food was inveterate. The food he provided was of a high quality, and resplendently served – his major-domo ensured that the table linen matched the dishes – and Jean Cocteau would sedulously partake of its pleasures.

Dior then bought 'La Colle Noire' near Caillan, and here too he carried out extensive alterations. When they were finished, he seemed to be living in the heart of a Roman villa.

And so it was that at Boussac's this highly valued and creative artist was offered all the credit he needed to satisfy his love of splendour, and his taste for beautiful houses and beautiful objects, a taste to which all else was sacrificed.

But the middle classes of Normandy are never totally blind to figures, and Dior was no exception. He understood the language of manufacturing and running costs, and knew the value of investments. He was always concerned to see his house well managed and judiciously expanded.

Dior's Paris home. Velvets, brocades, beautiful carpets and a rich variety of objects. *Photo by Maisons et Jardins.*

The bathroom in Paris, its taps designed especially for Dior.
Photo by Maisons et Jardins.

The small dining-room for intimate meals. Jean Cocteau was a frequent
guest. *Photo by Maisons et Jardins.*

La Colle Noire: the view was superb, and garden peas flourished.
Photo by Maywald.

La Colle Noire, Dior's second house. A Roman villa.

Lunch would be served in the garden. . . *Photo by Maywald.*

Christian Dior on the banks of his river. *Photo by Maywald.*

In his capacity as manager, Boussac had appointed Jacques Rouët to work with Dior as administrative director – a choice which seemed somewhat odd, since Rouët had come to fashion straight from the world of public service. When he first received him, Dior announced that the hat Rouët was wearing was quite impossible, and sent word that he should change it; but apart from this detail, he felt that here, perhaps, was the man for the job. He wanted an administrator from outside the world of high fashion, a man who was capable – in his own words – of showing both firm-handedness and diplomacy, in equal measure.

Rouët was very soon called upon to prove how effective he was. When Dior abducted Marguerite Carré from Patou (and with her a workshop of thirty women), and when he began to entice the best possible workers and sellers away from each and every atelier, a wailing and gnashing of teeth was heard through the land: Rouët was called on to arbitrate.

By the end of 1946 the manufacture of cloth was already beginning to pick up in Europe. Nevertheless it was with a supply of shantung, bought from the Chinese by Jacques Rouët, that the most famous model in the New Look collection was designed and made, a tailored suit by the name of 'Bar' comprising a black wool crêpe skirt and pale shantung jacket.

In the private world of the House of Dior, with its almost exclusively female workforce capable of showing every degree of devotion to duty, but hypersensitive to the atelier's highly charged atmosphere, and with a clientèle that was exclusively female and capable of every caprice and underhand cunning, Rouët was nonetheless able to introduce the maximum possible rationalization. It was Rouët, furthermore, who instituted the system of manufacturing garments under licence, a system from which couturiers drew the bulk of their income once they had managed to impose their trademark.

Dior never lost sight of how fragile a fashion house was, nor indeed of how fragile are all the things of this world. In the wake of the success of his second collection, Boussac wondered whether or not to exploit a name that had now assumed such a magical sound outside the field of high fashion itself. Dior was quickly convinced.

The first example of diversification was the opening in 1948 of a branch in New York selling luxury ready-to-wear goods. It was a wholly new concept. Two collections each year were created for American women to wear. Initially, Dior had the garments sewn in New York, but, distressed at the quality of the work produced there, he arranged for the stitching to be brought back to Paris.

It was after this that he opened a branch selling furs in the Avenue Montaigne, a shrine to sumptuous elegance.

Begun in 1949, the licensing system had started with stockings, the foot of which was designed by Dior himself to prevent the leg from twisting. His fellow couturiers thought such an activity vulgar and unworthy of a great designer, but this was a reproach which left him cold.

The last major investment for which Dior was responsible was the opening of the Grande Boutique in 1955. The Petite Boutique had been part of the original house in the Avenue Montaigne selling trinkets and fancy goods in an intimate atmosphere. Extending along the Rue François Ier, the Grande Boutique – the first of its kind – developed into a vast emporium that today contains more than six thousand items.

Dior had by now moved some distance away from being merely a competent tailor, devoting his talents to elegant women and polite society. A very great distance indeed. But his understanding of the age he lived in (in spite of his dislike for that age), the flexibility with which he adapted his (far from flexible) views, and the intuitive insight that he had of a future he feared – these are but different aspects of one and the same personality. He was an essentially intelligent man.

The Petite Boutique, decorated by Christian Bérard and selling fancy goods in an intimate setting.

The Grande Boutique, opened in 1955, a vast emporium stocking more than six thousand items. *Photos by Maywald.*

Roger Vivier, the shoe designer and the only man to enjoy the privilege of being Dior's co-signatory. *Photo by Maywald.*

Realizing a long-held dream of his, Dior was soon dressing women from head to toe, underclothing included. Ignorant only of how to make shoes, he entrusted their design to Roger Vivier.

Perfume completed his panoply of fashion. From his adolescence he had retained the delightful memory of a woman's perfume pervading the lift that he took to return to his rooms. 'Miss Dior' – so called in tribute to his sister – was the first such creation. It was the only domain where Dior himself was no innovator. Poiret, Chanel, Lanvin and Patou had their own makes already. But he made a success of it. The fashion house always remained the heart of the Dior Empire. There in the Avenue Montaigne twelve thousand items were produced every year, the very finest French products in terms of design and their realization.

Who was it who bought all these items? Three thousand women at most. Each current model, sold for 190,000 francs, was reproduced some forty times over, producing a profit of 12,000 francs each time it was copied. Only the most successful numbers achieved as many as 150 orders. Others were never asked for at all. It was a miniature industry when set beside the seven million dresses that are made and sold every year in France. But because it was Paris where this heart was beating, some eighty-seven countries throughout the world clamoured to sell dresses, stockings, girdles, brassières, swimsuits, ties, handbags, gloves, jewelry and shoes – all of them locally made – and to profit from the right to adopt so prestigious a name, as a result of the royalties they paid to one of ten companies set up in the name of Dior.

In addition to these, there were two firms that distributed perfume and lipstick in France and America; two branches in New York and London selling luxury ready-made models; and a branch in Caracas selling *haute couture*. Caracas was chosen because, thanks to the country's income from oil, Venezuelan women were counted among the world's wealthiest.

The future was no longer something to be feared. And yet, if the structure were not to collapse, its creator needed to recover his breath for each new season, to regain the power to enthral and astonish, so that two or three thousand Parisian women – who could as well be from Lyons or Lima – would want to wear a dress by Dior.

For a number of years Dior was able to derive fresh inspiration from within the style that had made him famous: he invented the calf-length, off-the-shoulder twilight dress, and the multiple pelisse made up of several detachable layers on a foundation of mink. He launched the dog collar, and never ceased to make new refinements. A case in point is the slit in tight skirts that is necessary to enable the wearer to walk: either it opens on the calf in a way that appears unseemly, or it opens on a fold which destroys the line of the skirt. In Dior's designs all skirts that formed part of a two-piece suit were mounted upon a taffeta sheath trimmed with a raised strip of the same material as the skirt itself, in such a way that the slit no longer revealed the wearer's legs, but only another skirt beneath. A tiny improvement which doubled the time that it took to produce each skirt.

But then, in 1954, having by now essayed all possible variants on the *Corolle* dress, Dior caused a new revolution. Assembled guests looked on in amazement as seven years of the New Look were wiped away in a mere three hours and replaced by the 'French Bean' woman. A change if ever there was one! And the moment was ripe. Following the inevitable rise and fall of every new fashion, the New Look had become perverted to the point of vulgarity. It deserved to perish.

Also known as the H Line or the 'Flat Look', the 'French Bean' woman was supremely elegant and supremely distinguished. She was also bustless, hipless and shoulderless – so much so that Marilyn Monroe declared herself insulted by the new design.

It may be added in passing that there is something quite comical about the way in which some women begin by opposing every new fashion, only to end up by showing an almost insane desire to adopt it for themselves, a characteristic already observed in his day by Poiret.

The press was divided and sometimes severe, especially in England. Dior was hurt but remarked philosophically, 'Better to be slated in three columns on the front page than congratulated in two lines on the inside pages.' What mattered most was that, once again, he was front-page

The youngest of Dior's clients, the two-year-old Caroline E., seen here in 1949 with the master himself.

news in all the world's papers as the result of reversing a trend that he himself had started.

Dior had to be tough to risk upsetting the world of French fashion through such an abrupt about-turn. But victory was his. As king of *haute couture*, Dior had acquired the weight that was needed to dictate what was fashionable.

Reaction against the New Look was discernible in other collections that season, as Balenciaga, Givenchy and Fath in turn made changes according to their own individual styles. But in the case of Dior the reaction compelled recognition, asserting itself as something already complete.

The same reaction was still to be seen the following seasons in liquid dresses, loosely fitting, that traced the simple outline of an adolescent ambiguity, flowing blouses, sliding belts, uncovered legs – but never the knee which Dior regarded as the ugliest part of a woman's body. His new collection marked the end of the high rounded bust, of the slender waist and curvaceous hips – over-direct and provincial ways of pleasing men. Fashion had found more subtle means of making women desirable. The cards in seduction's eternal game had been reshuffled.

At a later date, when Chanel re-emerged from her years of exile and caused a sensation with her famous suits, Dior was tickled pink by some of the things she would say: 'Balenciaga? He dresses women to look like old Spaniards! Dior? To look like armchairs. He puts covers over them!' Fashion is the sort of profession in which people take genuine pleasure in tearing each other apart. Dior's retort was sober by contrast. 'Chanel has created a fashion for elegant women rather than those who are pretty.' It was his last word on the subject.

It must be said that the two were not really rivals. Chanel's speciality, so to speak, was home-made confectionary, Dior's the creation of wedding cakes. Pungency and style meant more to Chanel than sound technique. It was enough for Dior to include a jersey cardigan in one of his last collections for certain observers to detect Chanel's influence. At most it was a tribute to her. No one could be said to exercise influence on Christian Dior, except the memory he retained of his mother. He knew what he wanted and forcibly carried it through, fighting within his domain to maintain those values that he saw to be crumbling elsewhere: 'In an age of machines, dressmaking has come to be the final refuge of all that is human, all that is personal, and all that can never be imitated.'

He also said, 'Dresses must have a soul.' Happily, he was able to persuade all who worked under him that this was so. His was an empire in which everyone, high or low, adored Dior because he had time for them; they respected him because, neither fickle nor moody, he stuck firmly to all his decisions; and they admired him simply for being the man that he was.

He loved his dresses as though they were people: they were his creatures until the day when they left his house. Then all that was left was to start all over again.

His work began with the simplest of tasks, the choice of suitable fabrics from among the many samples offered by manufacturers; only rarely did he make suggestions himself. Thus Madame Brossin de Méré, for example, who produced a number of excellent fabrics in Switzerland, was responsible for two materials that are still well-known, Sainte-gallette and Papillon. For the first of these it was a question of reproducing the harmonious colours of the roofs of St Gall, for the second, a light which Dior himself had asked her to capture.

Having ordered his fabrics, he would leave for the country and go off on holiday to clear his mind completely. Only then did he begin to draw, filling tiny sketchbooks with minuscule models. He scribbled things everywhere, in bed, in his bath, at table and in his car, capturing an emotion, a line or a movement. Suddenly one model among others

From left to right and front to back: The technical director Marguerite Carré; Christian Dior; the inspirational figure of Germaine Bricard; Jacques Rouët; Dior's guardian angel Raymonde Zehnacker; the sales director Suzanne Luling; the chief sales assistant Yvonne Minassian; Suzanne Begin; Madame Gervais; Monique, one of the head seamstresses; Madame Lancien, a sales assistant; Carmen Baron; Christiane Tisserand, another of the head seamstresses; Martine Priot, one of the sales assistants; and Nicole Rousseau.

would seize his attention – a theme he would then retain and develop. The very next morning another outline that had come to him during the night would in turn demand his attention. The sketches grew larger until he would stop 'like a pastrycook who, having kneaded his dough, will set it aside for a while'. After a week he would come back to the sketch, examine and simplify it, and then, in two or three days, make several hundred drawings on the strength of a dozen ideas.

The following stage found him back in the Avenue Montaigne, in a large bright studio where he always wore a white smock when working. It was here that his 'senior studio management' would meet, a famous trio of women – Madame Marguerite, mentioned earlier, Madame Raymonde and Madame Bricard.

Marguerite Carré had been one of the mainstays of Patou's firm when, on the advice of Georges Geffroy, Dior had enticed her away to become his technical director. She had a unique understanding of *haute couture*. Sure of her skills and fastidious to a fault, this impetuous, pink-faced woman was consumed by a veritable passion for dresses.

Madame Raymonde – Raymonde Zehnacker – had been poached from Lelong. What was her function? Her official title was head of management, but Dior called her his 'alter ego'. Mother, sister, governess, an exceptional organizer, and completely omniscient, Madame Raymonde was an angel. A blue-eyed guardian angel who could even tell fortunes by cards. She never left Dior; he would not have allowed her to do so. She shared an office with Jacques Rouët.

Germaine Bricard, for her part, was a quite astonishing woman. Legend has it that she had an affair with the Crown Prince of Germany. At all events she made no secret of having once been a *demi-mondaine* (as they say) or (if you prefer) a high-class tart. 'Nowadays,' she used to say, 'society women have brought the profession into disrepute. They'll go to bed for a *café crème*.'

Strictly speaking, clothes were her *raison d'être,* and she wore them with a real sense of style, inflexibly demanding in her sophistication. A consummate example of cosmopolitan elegance, according to Dior, she persisted in following a way of life that was all her own, rising at two in the afternoon, wearing a new dress every day, and resolved to 'hold out' to the end. Her moods and excesses, her comings and goings, her perpetual lateness, her views and remarks, and even her jewelry – she was someone quite out of the ordinary. Perhaps 'inspirational' is too strong a term; but it was a by no means minor role that Germaine Bricard played alongside Dior. She knew how to stimulate what he called his 'too rational temperament'. He had entrusted her with the hat department.

These three women councillors passed the sketches from hand to hand, commenting, judging, reacting. And in the light of their reactions Dior would reduce the number of sketches to some sixty or so, all of them variations upon a dozen themes. Madame Marguerite would then distribute the sketches among the various heads of department and seamstresses, who would then convert them into linen toiles.

One of these heads of department, in the early days, was a certain Monsieur Pierre. It was Pierre Cardin.

Then would come the most crucial day for the whole collection, when the 'Patron', armed with his gold-tipped cane, would examine the toiles with a critical eye.

Three models would wear them, none of them chosen at random from among the twelve or so 'jeunes filles' (as they are known in the trade) who worked in the fitting room.

Dior adored his models, and they felt the same about him. 'My models – they're the life of my dresses, and I want my dresses to be happy,' he said when his manager reproached him for paying the girls too much, when the head seamstresses expressed indignation at what they saw as Dior's indulgence towards them, and when his sellers declared that they could not put up with such girls.

The final rehearsal in the Grand Salon. Dior is seated between Germaine Bricard and Marguerite Carré, with Raymonde Zehnacker to the left. Jewels and accessories were chosen at this stage, buttons were changed, and everyone present would get involved. *Photo by Carone – Paris-Match.*

In his studio with Sylvie, one of his models. His predilection was for brunettes of average height. *Photo by Bellini.*

Working with Lucky, another of his models; in his hand the gold-tipped
cane with which he gave his instructions. *Photo by Bellini.*

He chose them himself, preferring brunettes of average height. But he drew a distinction between those of his girls who were merely successful, who shone in the salon and who knew how to 'carry' a dress, and those whom he called 'inspirational', with the gift of conveying a movement or outline while the dress was still at the toile stage.

It was three of these 'inspirational' models who presented the toiles from which he then made a final selection. By now all that was left were five or six basic types with their variations. He would then re-inspect each toile in turn and decide on the fabric in which the dress would be made, and on the girl who would wear it.

Certain designers derive their inspiration from fabrics when imagining their dresses, but this was never the case with Dior. He was described as an architect, and an architect does not build by draping his structures with curtains. 'To construct a series of volumes, proportionate to the female figure, in such a way as to highlight its forms', was how he understood his task, adding that in his eyes a collection could equally well be designed in black and white.

Above and beyond the subtle interplay of colour, it was the nature of his raw materials that commanded Dior's whole attention. Suppleness, firmness, thickness and weight – he would spend hour after hour considering these matters, 'a rite which would seem quite insane to the uninitiated,' he once wrote, 'and which consists in making the appropriate choice from among thirty high-quality black woollen fabrics.' Success depended upon the happy marriage of fabric and form.

All this, of course, was accompanied by restless activity, shouting and tension, and by the feverish excitement that is an inescapable part of *haute couture*. In the course of a further session, all the toiles that deserved to be modelled were recorded, filed and baptized – 'Amoureuse', 'Gigolo', 'Paltoquet', 'Gala', 'Blandine'. In every collection a suit called 'Bobby' evoked the memory of the Patron's dog.

And every collection included a dress that was red – Dior's lucky colour – with plenty of black because, as he said, 'the violent accent of black makes it the most elegant colour.'

The toiles were returned to the workrooms and transformed into dresses, this time made in the chosen fabric. And then came their very first showing, in the presence of Dior himself, and following an unchanging ritual.

'Monsieur, a model. . .': the announcement was made as each new design made its entrance; Dior needed this theatrical setting. The model twirled around. And then, in the company of Madame Marguerite and one of the head seamstresses, or the tailor and seamstress in charge of the dress, Dior would work on the model, lengthening it here, shortening it there, lowering the neckline, or laying the dress out flat and moving a seam by a centimetre.

The following stage took place in the Grand Salon beneath crystal chandeliers. It was here that some thirty finished models would file past their creator, chosen from among the most representative examples; and, of these, Dior would indicate the ones that were destined to found a new line, those whose principles he wished to affirm and whose consequences he wished to prolong.

In the end, each collection – 175 models plus coats to go with them – was made up of a predetermined number of suits, day dresses, evening dresses and coats, and a necessary number of models that it was assumed would sell well, such as those spectacular numbers christened 'Trafalgars'. But there was always a strict consistency to every collection.

It was complete by the day of the final rehearsal when all that remained was for a few cosmetic improvements to be made. Removing or adding a button, changing a gemstone, replacing a belt, altering a hat – everyone was involved at this stage, and it was often midnight before the session was over.

Dior taking a final look at Olivia de Haviland's dress, created for the film
The Ambassador's Daughter.

For Ava Gardner, Dior was exceptionally attentive.

From time to time a model would pass by, irreproachable from head to toe, and Dior would murmur, 'How pretty she is! Couldn't be better dressed. Couldn't be more elegant!' And all around him voices rang out, 'Just like a painting!' In the language of *haute couture*, painting is synonymous with perfection.

On days like this, as he sat in an armchair, his pockets bulging with rubbers and pencils, waving his cane like some theatre director at work with his cast, Dior was a happy man. But the very next morning he was consumed by anxiety.

When seen as a whole, each collection was an opulent spectacle that evoked the kind of emotion only pure beauty is apt to inspire. On one such occasion a woman was so deeply moved that she went down to a neighbouring florist and asked for the entire shop to be sent to Dior, just as a bouquet of flowers might be thrown to a famous soprano. In order that the performance might pass off to greatest possible effect on the day of the première, a whole ceremonial was brought into play, with the general public – some three hundred people – subtly divided between the Grand Salon and the Petit Salon, and bursting into applause at just the right moment so that others might follow them. Of course, attendance on such an occasion was by invitation only. This was as a point of principle, but also because of Dior's obsessive fear that he might be copied; his paranoia was so great that he once physically ejected a woman whom he caught in the act of sketching one of his models. As for the buyers, they paid a deposit, forfeited in the event of their failure to place any orders.

The morning session was reserved for the press, the afternoon one for a hand-picked audience, chosen by Dior himself. The buyers arrived the following day, and private customers three weeks later.

A childhood friend of Dior's from Granville, a tall, inexhaustible woman by the name of Suzanne Luling, reigned over the salons and over

To the left of the picture the Duchess of Windsor. She was on the list of women one had to dress. *Photo by Maywald.*

André Maurois and his wife, two of the hand-picked members of the afternoon session. *Photo by Maywald.*

relations with customers. Exuberant and noisy, she knew her job like the back of her hand; she could dance and drink all night with the horde of American buyers whom she entertained at her home decorated with gilded panelling, to the sound of the band from 'Jimmy's', and arrive at work intact at 9 o'clock the next morning.

Even before the doors of the shop had been opened, she and Dior had drawn up a list of the women they wanted to dress. For the most part these women were foreign. Invited to Paris, they had almost all placed orders. More important than that, they had all come back. Marlene Dietrich, the Duchess of Windsor, Lady Mendl, Patricia Lopez Willshaw. . . And many others had followed, both from France and abroad. A whole series of well-to-do women whose names were unknown, but in whose eyes the House of Dior had become an institution; from the moment they placed their first orders, there was no further question of going elsewhere. This strange phenomenon was hard to explain except by recalling the firm's beginnings: Dior was fashion, Dior was Paris, Dior was reliability and good taste.

To say that all of these women were elegantly dressed when leaving Dior would be telling a lie. There was also the question of style and of personal talent, factors that cannot be quantified. But what one can say is that all the elegant women of the day bought their clothes from Dior at one time or another, excepting only the mad millionairesses who would order the whole of a single collection. One can also say that, from the wedding dress worn by Princess Margaret and the little black dress of Edith Piaf to the evening dresses of Madame Auriol, the French President's wife, every woman who was ever in the public eye passed the length of the Avenue Montaigne.

Some fifty experienced saleswomen were skilled at helping their customers to make the right choice and at discouraging incautious excesses by saying, 'I do not like you in that one.' A difficult thing to have to say! But a good assistant is one who sells a dress that the client feels happy to wear. The rule at Dior's was never to rush a hesitant customer. 'Let her go elsewhere, she'll come back in the end,' Suzanne Luling used to say.

Countess Greffulhe: after the 1947 collection she was heard to remark, 'It's very good, what little Christian's doing.'

Opposite: The staircase crowded for the 1955 opening. In spite of the lack of space, a chair was found for Marlene Dietrich.
Photos by Maywald.

The battalion of sales assistants on the day of the opening. There would soon be fifty of them in all. *Photo by Louise Dahl-Wolfe.*

A couturier's customers inevitably include a number of women who can only be described as a pain in the neck – women who have no idea what they want, who are never satisfied, and who think they can haggle. The House of Dior had its share of such women. But Dior refused to allow them to insult his assistants. Although he never attended a fitting, he once made an exception for an important client who, for some reason or other, had expressed her dissatisfaction. But when he heard the tone of voice in which she addressed his head seamstress, he asked the woman to leave. It was as simple as that.

As for the foreign buyers – a breed which has all but disappeared in an age when the whole of the fashion industry has moved over to ready-made gowns – these people worshipped Dior. In its earliest years the House of Dior alone accounted for 75 per cent of French fashion exports. In financial terms the buyers were the most important clients since they paid a surcharge of 40 to 50 per cent on each model they bought; thus they acquired the right to make copies, buying the garment without trying it on and often even in the form of a toile or a paper pattern. Wholesalers would come to observe, to feel the dresses and to make calculations. Above all else they would read the papers before risking any deposit; hence the importance attached to press reactions. If Carmel Snow fell into a doze, or if Eugenia Sheppard of the *Herald Tribune* were to chat to her neighbour, there was cause for alarm, for both of these women had infallible judgment.

But as a general rule the press show was punctuated by applause, right up to the spectacular final *coup* when the bridal dress was presented amidst hugging and kissing and effusive remarks such as 'sublime, divine and simply ravishing'; an ordeal, perhaps, but it marked the pinnacle of the creator's achievements. A little flushed, Dior would emerge from the models' changing room where, as though in a trance, he had watched his dresses float away. Some two hundred women would seek to embrace

Japanese women capitulated at the sight of the Y Line, represented here
by a two-piece dress with tweed coat. 1955.

The Duchess of Marlborough, with Philippe de Rothschild to the right of
the picture. *Photos by Maywald.*

him; perhaps fifty succeeded. He allowed it to happen, delighted, relieved and content.

Perfect clothes worn by perfect models in a perfect setting – how good if the spectacle could have ended like that, like a ballet performed but a single time for a fairy-tale prince. But a fashion house is a business. These well-loved dresses and much-adored clothes, so exquisitely cut to fit the figure of Renée, Allah or Victoire, so beautifully embroidered to suit Sylvie, so prettily sewn to hug France – these dresses began to be passed around, to be turned over and over in the large and ungainly hands of buyers anxious to copy them, and tried on by women only too keen to be seen inside them. The inevitable wear and tear that was suffered by these beautiful objects, products of such love and such skill, this trivialization of Dior's dresses was a source of distress to him. He could not bear to watch; he left. He never saw the same collection twice.

By contrast, he liked to see his dresses copied and worn by those of his friends whom he thought of as elegant, and as a result a number of these women had the privilege of being dressed by Dior without having the means to afford it. He merely entreated them – unsuccessfully – to wear matching gloves and a hat.

He scarcely had use for an assistant designer when a fashion design competition was organized in 1953 by people involved in textile manufacture. The winner was a tall young man of seventeen, his periwinkle-blue eyes hidden behind a large pair of glasses. The jury was headed by Michel de Brunhoff, director of *Vogue*. 'You must take him on,' he told Dior.

Dior obeyed him. The young man in question, a timid and delicate youth, came from Oran in Algeria, where his father worked in insurance. His name was Yves Mathieu Saint Laurent.

So gifted was he that Dior appointed him as his assistant. It was the first time that anyone had ever assisted him at the initial design stage.

A collar that holds its shape. 1950. *Photo by Irving Penn.*

Though granted so soon, the privilege of working with Dior did not prevent Saint Laurent from growing painfully bored in so vast a house where, in spite of everything, he was well liked for his touching appearance; he only looked about twelve, and was prone to headaches.

But he worked so well that one day in October 1957, Dior went to Jacques Rouët's office and told him, 'I've made up my mind. There are thirty models in my latest collection that are based on Saint Laurent's designs. He is an exceptional talent. He's been working beside me for eighteen months. I want the papers to know all about him; I want him to be recognized; I want justice to be done to him.'

'But he's not yet twenty,' Jacques Rouët and Madame Raymonde exclaimed at once. 'Wait just a little longer.'

'No,' Dior answered. 'I won't wait. I want it done by next time.'

But there was no next time.

A few days later Dior left for Montecatini to follow a course of treatment there. On 24 October 1957 at midnight he complained of feeling unwell. A priest was called. . . Then silence. He was fifty-two.

An aeroplane from Boussac's fleet took off at once with Madame Raymonde, Jacques Rouët, one of the firm's administrators and Dior's doctor on board. On the return flight, when they tried to get the coffin inside, they discovered that it was too long. It had to be carried in a standing position.

The death of the world's most famous couturier was felt as a real calamity. The sense of emotion was great, as shock waves passed round the world; thousands upon thousands of lilies of the valley – his favourite flower – were strewn on his bier; a crowd of mourners jostled for space on the pavement outside his parish church of Saint-Honoré-d'Eylau, and during the service an anthem was played that was specially written by his very dear friend Henri Sauguet; he was buried at Caillan, in the village cemetery, in the earth to which he felt closest.

The career of the prince of elegance, Christian Dior, had come to an end.

What remains of him? A name whose lustre seems incorruptible, a name that throughout the long years has retained not only its commercial pulling power but also its power to conjure up dreams – a name writ in letters of gold.

Beyond that? Beautiful memories on the part of a handful of women who were loved for the dresses they wore.

And finally? An intangible something. The gossamer trail that is left on this earth by all architects of the ephemeral.

Françoise Giroud

Opposite: Christian Bérard and his dog, with Renée, one of the models. Bérard was one of Dior's earliest friends, from the days when he used to sell paintings. *Photo by Richard Avedon.*

The 1947 look – a chignon at one side of the head, a tambourin hat on the other. *Photo by Louise Dahl-Wolfe.*

Opposite: Hollow waist and rounded hips – a New Look coat in black wool crêpe. 1947. *Photo by Louise Dahl-Wolfe.*

Made for walking rather than sitting, this black-and-white hound's-tooth
dress marked the *Envol* or 'Take-Off' Line. 1948.

Opposite: The 'Zigzag' Line in grey flannel. 1948. *Photo by Coffin.*

Small two-piece from the spring 1949 collection in grey pepper-and-salt
over a white piqué blouse. *Photo by Maywald.*

'Acacias', a classic line in grey wool from the 1949 collection.
Photo by Maywald.

A large and ample coat in coarse, untreated iron-grey wool, fastened by a
single button. 1950. *Photo by Pottier.*

Opposite: Travelling coat in coarse buff wool worn over a shirtwaister
and known as 'Sandman'. 1949.

'Shepherd boy' – a black ottoman paletot with lapels buttoned at
the back. 1949.

Opposite: 'Pentecost', coarse silk jacket with horseshoe lapels and
belted over a tight-fitting sheath dress. 1950. *Photos by Maywald.*

Opposite: A three-quarter length black wool jacket fastened by a black satin knot. 1950. *Photo by Irving Penn.*

Page 112 A black wool wasp-waisted coat: everything is in the collar. 1950. *Photo by Irving Penn.*

Page 113 A flared sheath in grey wool crêpe, lightened by a pocket handkerchief and three rows of pearls. 1950. *Photo by Irving Penn.*

Dress and loose-fitting coat in white cloth with a huge beaver lapel; muff
and hat in beaver fur. 1950. *Photo by Pottier.*

Opposite: Double-breasted two-piece suit in black wool crêpe with an
accentuated basque. 1950. *Photo by Irving Penn.*

A jewel of a little hat. 1950. *Photo by Louise Dahl-Wolfe.*

Opposite: Dog collar and pink satin hat adorned by a pendant pearl.
Photo by Sacha.

A small wasp-waisted two-piece in grey wool crêpe. 1950.
Photo by Pottier.

Opposite: 'Slyboots' is a beige shantung spencer worn over a sheath with
a lacquered belt. 1951. *Photo by Pottier.*

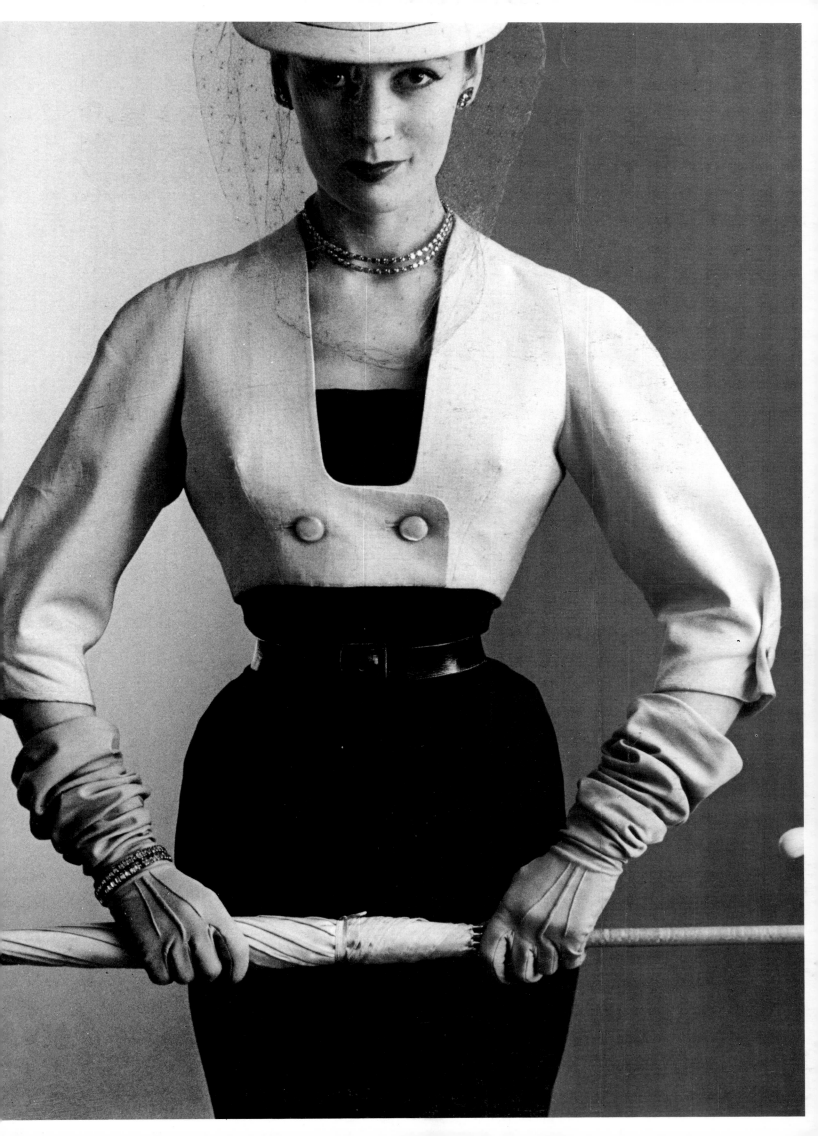

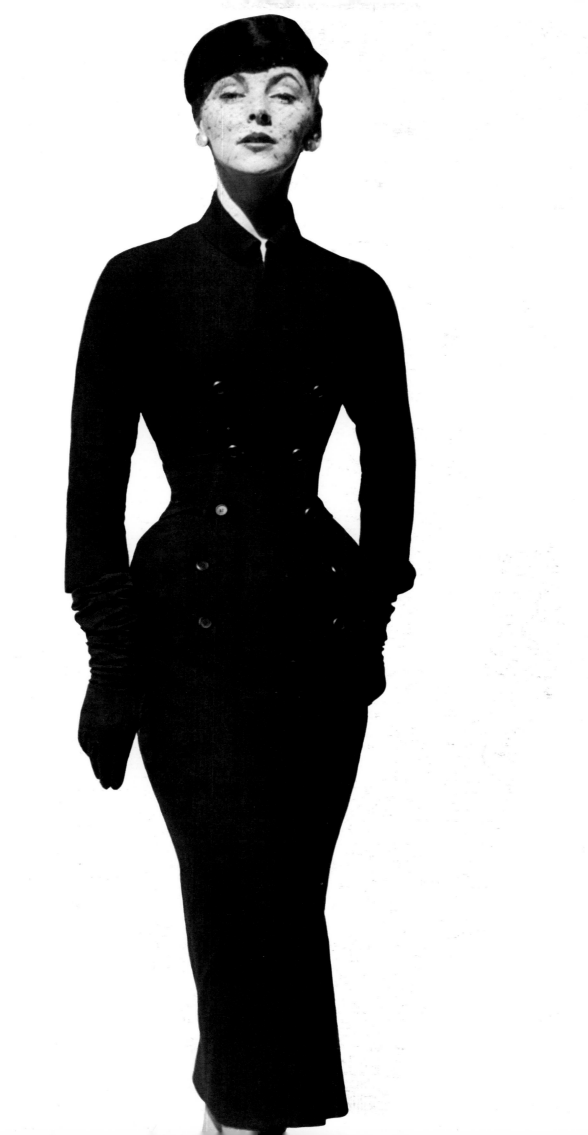

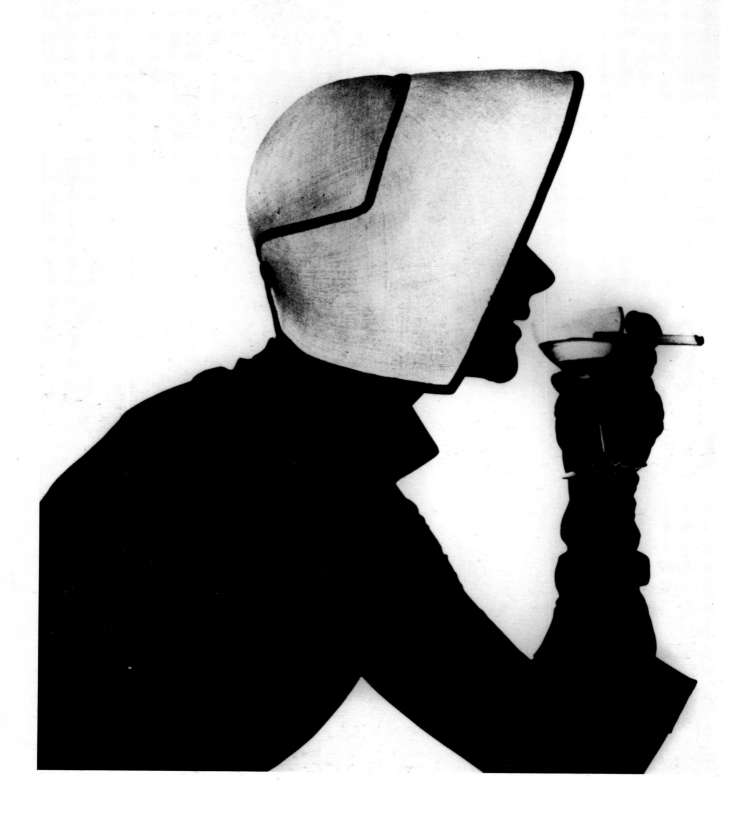

What counts in a hat is its profile. . . 1952 and 1953.
Photos by Irving Penn (left) and Pottier (right).

The H Line in black wool crêpe, an ensemble that broke with seven years
of variations on the New Look. 1954.

Opposite: A two-piece suit in Cordoba wool, worn with a silver fox fur
muff. 1954. *Photo by Maywald.*

This page and opposite: 'Surprise' – the Y Line in black satin shantung.
1955. *Photos by Sacha.*

Page 135   The A Line – a two-piece in iron-grey wool crêpe. 1955.
Photo by Sacha.

Page 138   A reversible ocelot paletot. 1957. *Photo by Sacha.*

Page 139   A patchwork of speckled furs for a coat made in 1976.
Photo by Sacha.

Pages 142 and 143   A golden chinchilla jacket lined with ostrich
feathers. 1984. *Photo by Sacha.*

A generously cut natural mink coat with soft collar and three-quarter
length sleeves. 1954. *Photo by Louise Dahl-Wolfe.*

Opposite: A coat in Emba mink, the first perfectly white variety of
mink. 1948. *Photo by Maywald.*

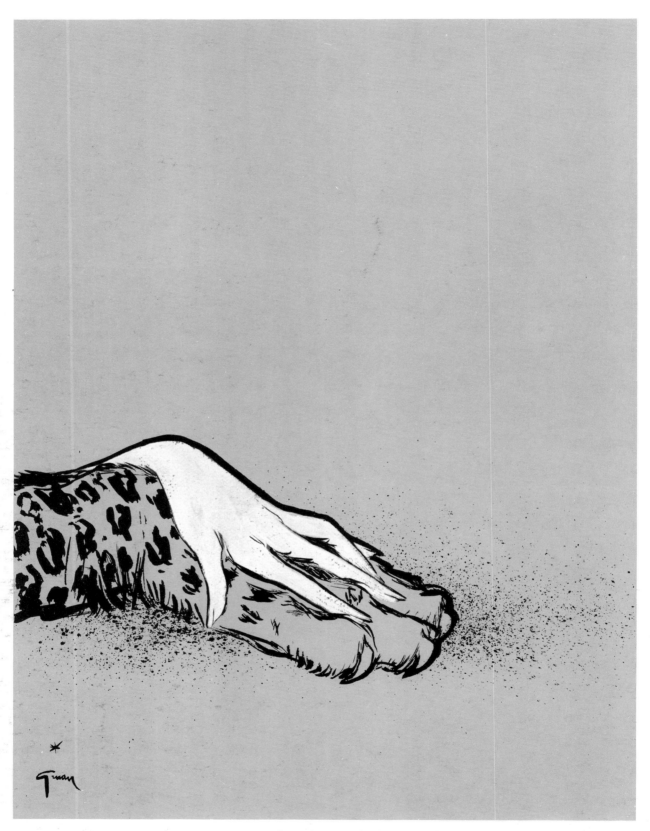

Gruau's design for 'Miss Dior'. 1948.

Opposite: The inspirational figure of Germaine Bricard, inflexibly demanding in her sophistication. *Photo by Cecil Beaton.*

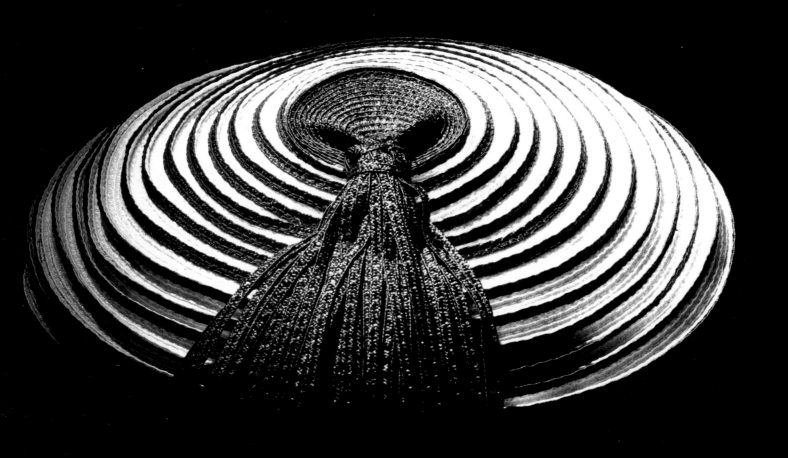

A boater. *Photo by Sacha.*

Opposite: A trim little hat, with a tassel. *Photo by Sacha.*

Jaqueline

Ida
160

Ida

Marcelle

Braided silk tambourin hat. 1955. *Photo by Sacha.*

Pages 150, 151, 153, 154 and 155   The first stage: scale drawings by Monsier Dior.

Shanghai

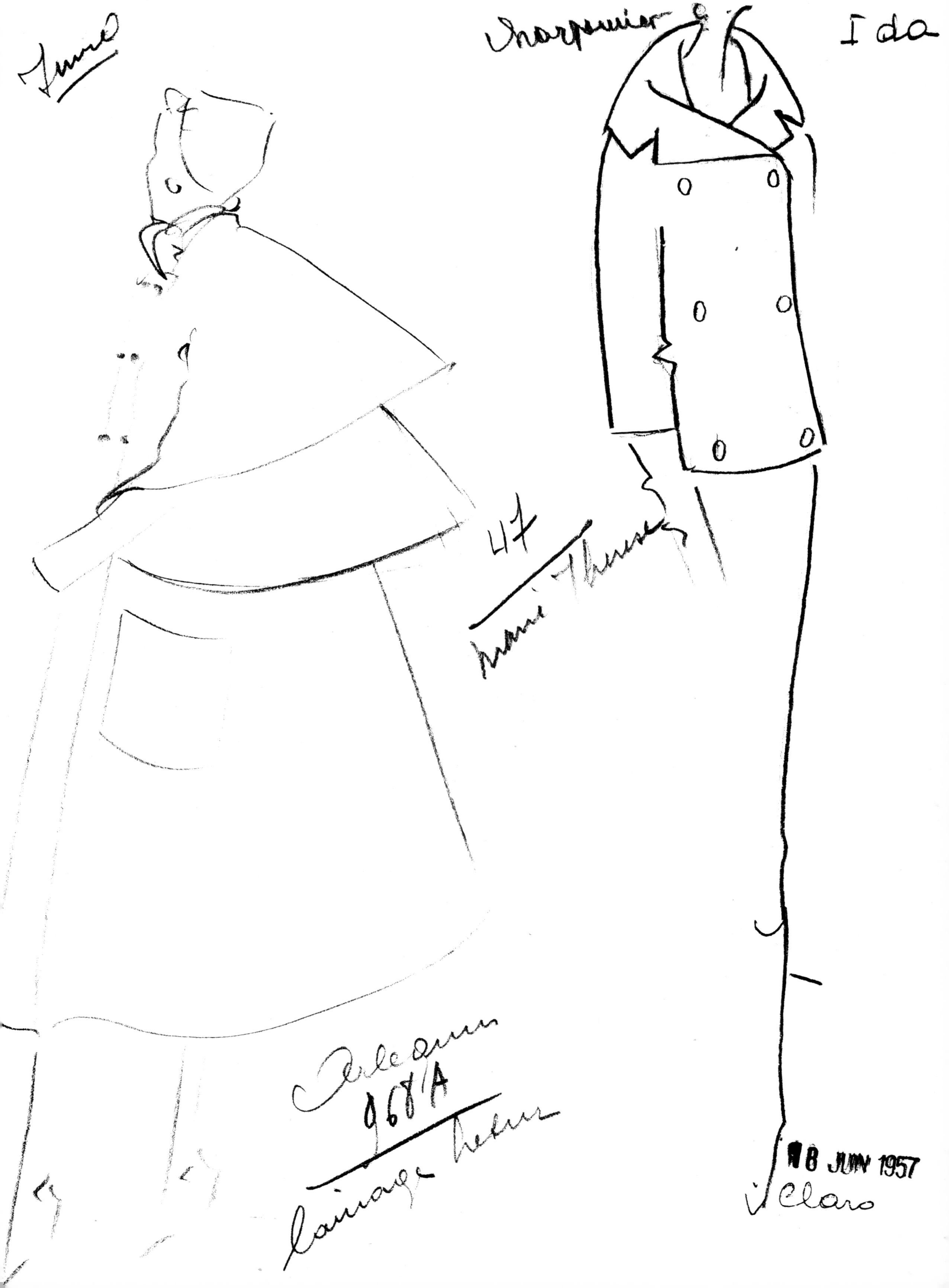
Charpentier
Ida
47
968 A
8 JUIN 1957

The 'Miss Dior' perfume bottle.

'Miss Dior' eau de toilette. 1948. *Photo by Maywald.*

Page 159 'Promise', an austere model in black wool crêpe. 1957.
Photo by Sacha.

'Miss Dior' in a crystal amphora. 1947.

Opposite: Refill for 'Miss Dior' atomizer. 1948. *Photo by Maywald.*

Gruau's design for advertising 'Diorama' perfume. 1955.

Opposite: Gruau's design for Dior perfume. 1956.

Gruau's design for Dior. 1949.

Gruau's design for 'Miss Dior'. 1947.

Gruau's design for 'Eau Sauvage'. 1980.

Opposite: Gruau's publicity for 'Dior' perfume. 1978.

Gruau's design for 'Miss Dior'. 1949.

Opposite: Dedicated to Francis Poulenc, this exercise in virtuosity was
made of pleated taffeta. 1950. *Photo by Maywald.*

Opposite: A handful of roses and a mass of pearl-coloured satin on a tulle
evening dress. 1947. *Photo Louise Dahl-Wolfe.*

'Cyclone': charcoal black taffeta for a dance-dress. 1948.

Opposite: 'Midnight' – warm brown velvet embroidered with black diamonds for a short cabaret dress. 1948. *Photo by Maywald.*

A profusion of stripes for a long organdie dress. 1948. *Photo by Sacha.*

The graceful elegance of a piece of jewelry on a black velvet cap. 1949.
Photo by Louise Dahl-Wolfe.

Opposite: An emerald ringed with cabochon rubies mounted on a silver
swan fringed with pearls. *Photo by Sacha.*

For the 'demi-soir', a large navy-blue satin coat worn over a velvet dress of
the same colour. 1949.

Opposite: 'Carnavalet', a full black taffeta evening dress with an
enormous collar. 1949. *Photos by Maywald.*

Two black sheath dresses with diagonal lines, mixing velvet with satin.
1949. *Photo by Horst.*

'Marly', an evening dress in golden yellow faille, in the Trompe-l'oeil Look.
Photo by Maywald.

For a Venetian ball, two full black-and-white evening dresses. 1952.
Photo by Henry Clarke.

Opposite: 'Schumann', a white chiffon evening dress trimmed with
several rows of ribbon. 1950. *Photo by Louise Dahl-Wolfe.*

A sketch by Bernard Blossac of one of Dior's New Look models.

30 Avenue Montaigne as seen by Christian Bérard. 1947.

Mary Jane Russell wearing a polka-dot cocktail dress.
Photo by Louise Dahl-Wolfe.

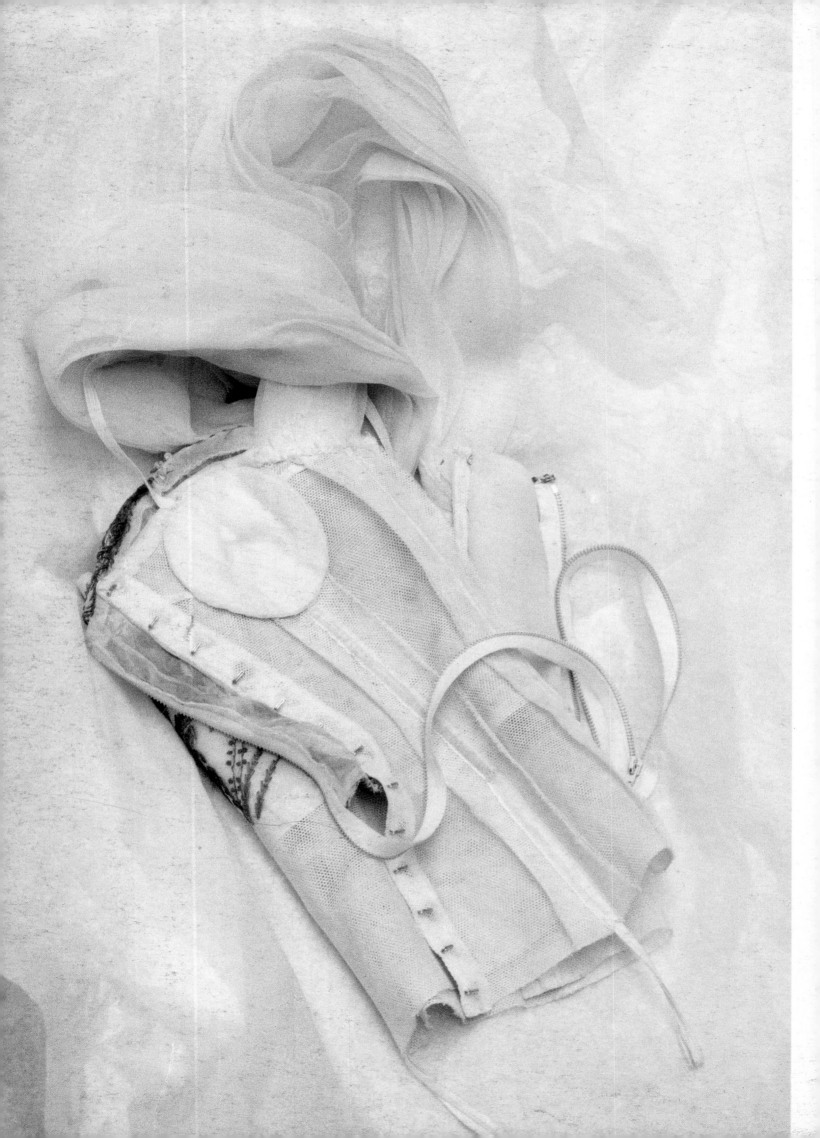

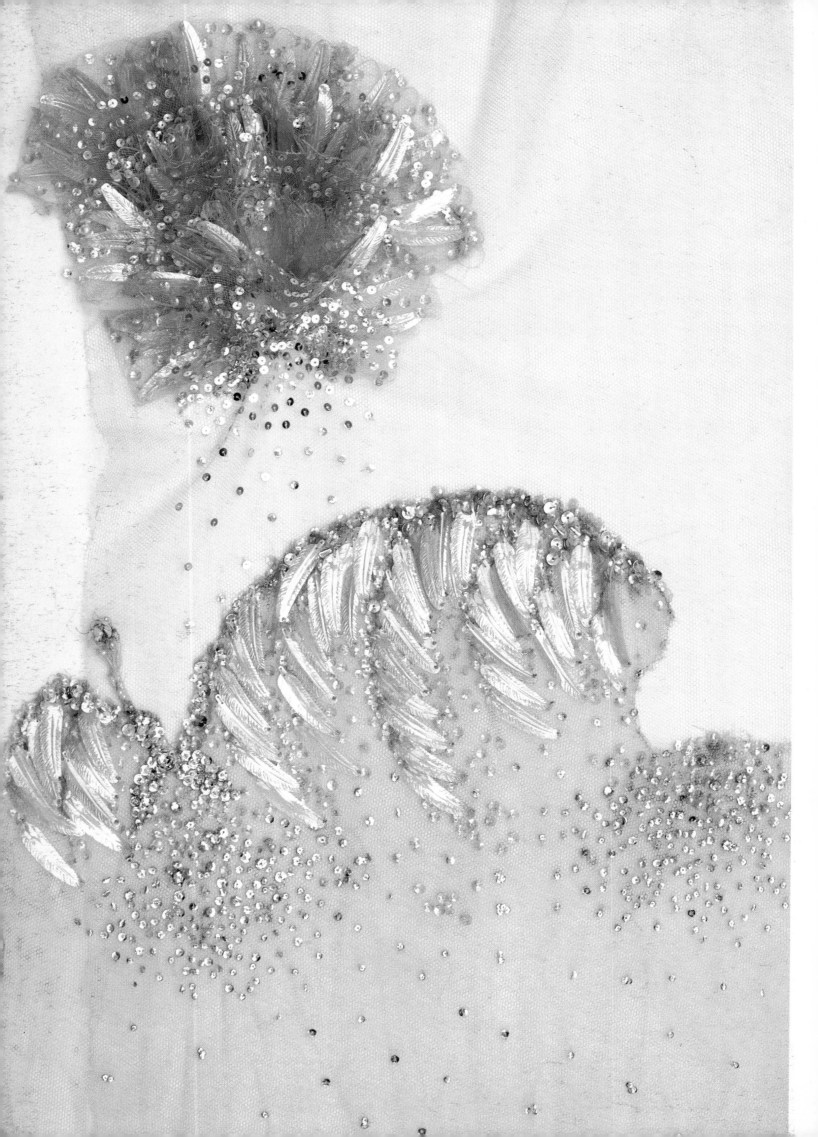

An off-the-shoulder dress in pale pink satin, with matching paletot and a
coil of satin as a headdress. 1952.

Opposite: Day dress in watered, textured ottoman. 1952.
Photos by Frances MacLaughlin.

A pleated day dress in white crêpe. 1952.

Opposite: Matt gold, blue and pink gemstones (above), spheres of
unburnished gold and iridescent stones (below). *Photo by Sacha.*

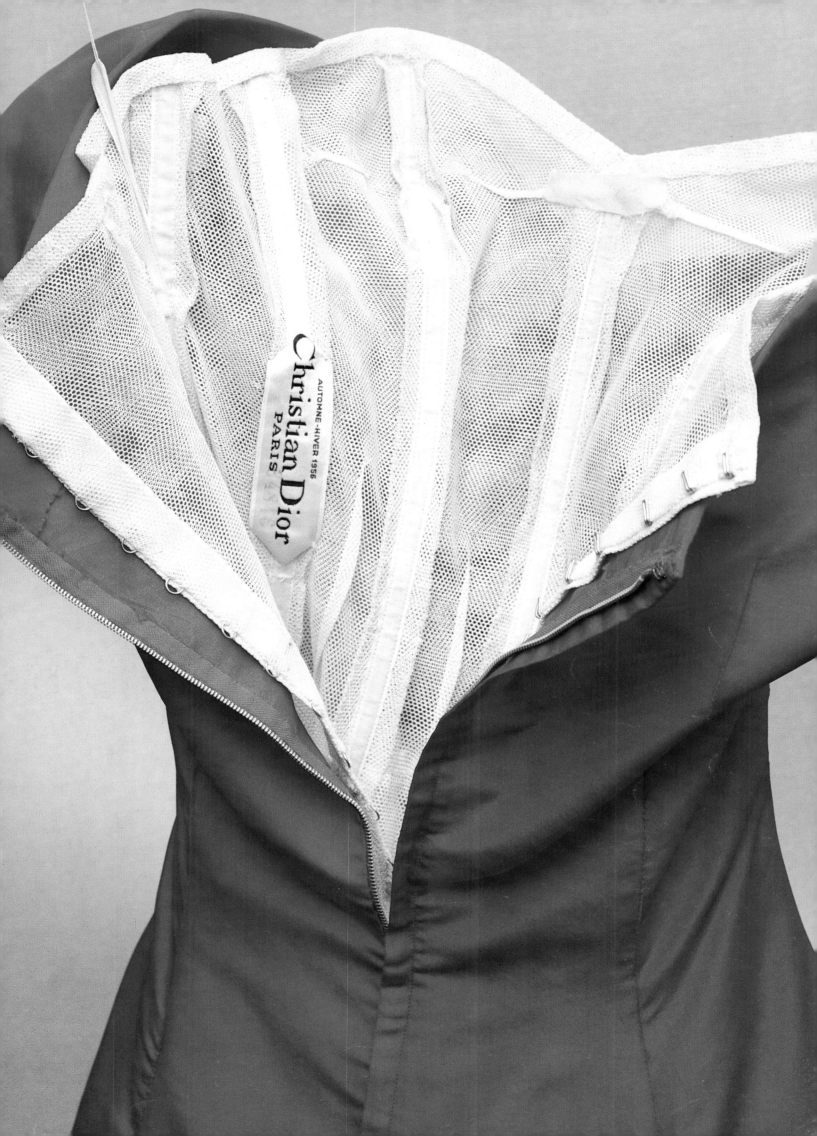

Black silk faille cocktail dress with white fichu. 1955. *Photo by Pottier.*

Printed taffeta cocktail dress with roundel motif. 1955. *Photo by Pottier.*

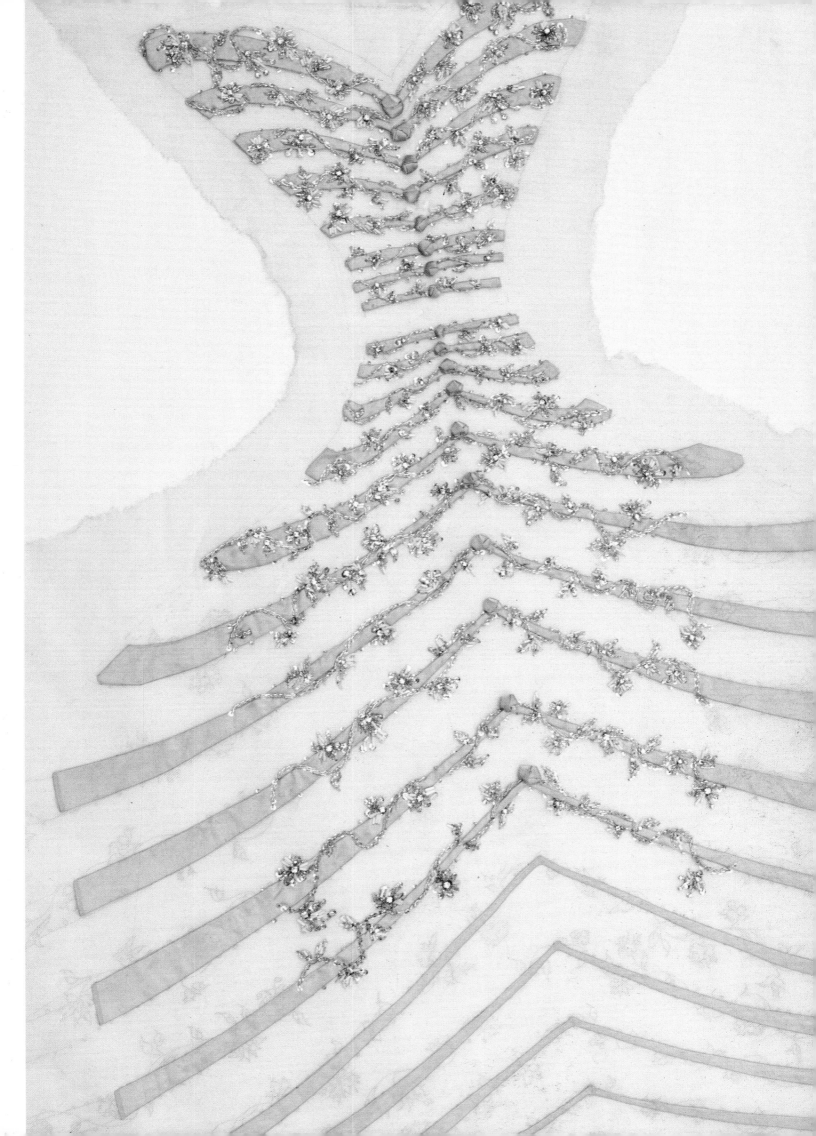

A slightly showy cocktail dress in white taffeta printed with yellow and pink roses. 1956. *Photo by Kublin.*

Opposite: 'Istanbul' or 'Sheherazade', a calf-length evening dress in gold and pink brocade. 1956. *Photo by Maywald.*

Knotted satin for cocktail wear. 1956. *Photo by Norman Parkinson.*

Opposite: The lustre of mother-of-pearl embroidered on a white satin
dress. *Photo by Sacha.*

'Black Swan', ostrich feathers on white taffeta. 1957. *Photo by Sacha.*

A menu designed by Dior in January 1940.

Opposite: In his garden at the Moulin. He had green fingers.
Photo by Ostier.

Christian DIOR
30, Avenue Montaigne - PARIS-8e
Croquis N° 85
18 JUIN 1957

The pleasure of drowning in a low-cut black silk faille dress. 1957.
Photo by Guy Bourdin.

Opposite: Another black taffeta dress with plunging neckline, just
brushing the top of the shoulders. 1957. *Photo by Guy Bourdin.*

Design by Christian Dior for one of the costumes in Roland Tual's film
Le Lit à colonnes.

Opposite: A costume inspired by Edouard Manet for a fancy-dress ball
given by Les Noailles. 1956. *Photo by Sacha.*

One of the five best-known men in the world. *Photo by Maywald.*

Opposite: Dior's 'girls' in 1957. *Photo by Loomis Dean – Life.*

The heir apparent, Yves Saint Laurent, in 1957.

Pages 272, 273 and 274   Saint Laurent designed these three evening
gowns before leaving to do his military service.

Marc Bohan Collections.

Dior's successor, Marc Bohan, in 1959.

The ever-faithful Diana Vreeland. *Photo by Hatami.*

Marc Bohan being congratulated by Danielle Darrieux after the spring–
summer 1963 fashion parade. *Photo by Hatami.*

DIOR AFTER DIOR
A NAME WRIT IN LETTERS OF GOLD

Thirty years after the death of Christian Dior, the empire which he founded continues to prosper. Having been caught up for a time in the upheavals suffered by Boussac, it is now in the hands of the holding company Agache. Only the perfume business has become a separate concern, having been sold to the Moët-Hennessy group in 1968. For the rest, the Dior Empire is now made up as follows:

One million ready-to-wear items produced annually, of which 600,000 are sold in the United States of America and 300,000 in Japan.

A total volume of business of nearly six thousand million francs, 93 per cent of which derives from articles manufactured under licence.

Two hundred manufacturing agreements with twenty-five countries throughout the world – from West Germany to Zimbabwe – and covering some fifty different articles.

Thirty shops: in Paris, Geneva, Buenos Aires, Singapore, Taipei, Riyadh, Monaco, Beirut, Hong Kong, Osaka, Basle, Madrid, etc.

An *Haute Fourrure* division selling furs, under the management of Frédéric Castet; both in development and reputation this division post-dates 1968 and now has an annual turnover of 25 million francs.

Finally, the *Haute Couture* division, necessary to the label's prestige but representing only 47 million francs, or less than 1 per cent of the company's total volume of business. The *Haute Couture* division produces around 8000 items a year, at an average price of between 46,000 and 58,000 francs.

Following Dior's death in October 1957, Yves Saint Laurent ensured that a further six collections were designed and created before he began his military service in 1960. He was replaced as artistic director by Marc Bohan, who continues to fill this post today.

From left to right: Jacques Rouët, Marcel Boussac and Marc Bohan.

Dior at his desk. There were five generations of industrialists behind him.

DIOR IN 22 LINES

1947
Spring – Summer   COROLLE AND 8

1948
Spring – Summer   ZIGZAG AND ENVOL (Take-Off)
Autumn – Winter   CYCLONE

1949
Spring – Summer   TROMPE-L'OEIL
Autumn – Winter   MILIEU DU SIÈCLE (Mid-Century)

1950
Spring – Summer   VERTICALE
Autumn – Winter   OBLIQUE

1951
Spring – Summer   NATURELLE
Autumn – Winter   LONGUE

1952
Spring – Summer   SINUEUSE
Autumn – Winter   PROFILÉE (Streamlined)

1953
Spring – Summer   TULIPE
Autumn – Winter   VIVANTE (Alive)

1954
Spring – Summer   MUGUET (Lily of the Valley)
Autumn – Winter   H LINE

1955
Spring – Summer   A LINE
Autumn – Winter   Y LINE

1956
Spring – Summer   FLÈCHE (Arrow)
Autumn – Winter   AIMANT (Magnet)

1957
Spring – Summer   LIBRE (Free)
Autumn – Winter   FUSEAU (Spindle)

At about the age of ten. Even then he did not like change.

Christian Dior and his brother Bernard at Granville. Well behaved and well brought up.

A group of children on the beach at Granville, with Christian
among them.

Back row (left to right): Christian, Jacqueline, Bernard and Raymond.

Front row (left to right): Madame Madeleine Dior, Catherine and
Monsieur Maurice Dior.

CHRONOLOGY

1905. Born at Granville on the English Channel on 21 January – the anniversary of the death of Louis XVI, as Dior was fond of recalling.

1910. The Dior family – Raymond, Christian, Jacqueline, Bernard, Catherine and their mother – move to Paris to take up residence in the Rue Albéric Magnard, then known as the Rue Richard Wagner. (Its name was changed during the First World War.) The family moves several times during the years that follow, but remains within the district of Passy. Christian studies at the Ecole Tannenberg to take his *baccalauréat*.

1923. Christian Dior follows a course in political science, studies musical composition, and develops an enthusiastic interest in the works of Les Six. His friends at this time include Henri Sauguet, Christian Bérard, Pierre Gaxotte and Jean Ozenne.

1927. Dior on military service as a private sapper with the Fifth Engineers of Versailles.

1928. Dior and his friend Jacques Bonjean open an art gallery in the Rue de la Boétie.

1931. Death of Dior's mother. Following the stock exchange crash of 1929 and unfortunate investments, his father finds himself financially ruined. The young Dior leaves for the Soviet Union with a group of architects, and on his return learns that his partner Jacques Bonjean has also been ruined. He sells off the paintings in his gallery and joins Pierre Colle. But it is a time of crisis for Dior: he is utterly destitute.

1934. Dior falls gravely ill and has to leave Paris for a year.

1935. Jean Ozenne offers him a roof over his head, and initiates him into the world of fashion design. Dior soon sells his first sketches for dresses and hats, and among his customers is the milliner Agnès.

1937. Georges Geffroy introduces him to Robert Piguet, who buys some of his designs. He works for the fashion pages of *Le Figaro*.

1938. Piguet opens a fashion house at the Rond-Point on the Champs-Elysées, and takes on Dior as a designer.

1939. Dior is called up and posted to Mehun-sur-Yèvre.

1940. Demobilized, Dior rejoins his father and sister Catherine at Caillan in the Var, where he takes up farming.

1941. At the end of 1941 he returns to Paris, where his place at Piguet's has already been taken by Antonio de Castillo. Lucien Lelong takes him on.

1946. With the financial backing of Marcel Boussac, Dior leaves Lelong and founds his own fashion house in a small private mansion at 30 Avenue Montaigne. Victor Grandpierre is responsible for the interior design. From now on Dior's name is associated with the colour combination of pearl-grey and white. The firm is run by Jacques Rouët.

1947. On 12 February Dior presents his first collection – ninety models worn by six girls. The lines are called 'Corolle' and '8' but are very soon re-christened 'the New Look'.
Dior receives a fashion award from Neimann-Marcus in Dallas, and seizes the opportunity to travel around the United States, where factions spring up against 'the man who hides women's legs'.
The Christian Dior perfume company is set up under the control of Serge Heftler Louiche. Dior christens the first perfume 'Miss Dior' in tribute to his sister.
He buys the Moulin du Coudret near Milly-la-Forêt, and later that year leaves his apartment in the Rue Royale for a small private mansion in the Boulevard Jules Sandeau in Passy.
Pierre Cardin starts work with Dior as the head of one of his ateliers, remaining with the firm until 1950.

1948. In November a fashion house selling luxury ready-to-wear items is opened in New York at the corner of Fifth Avenue and 57th Street. Known as Christian Dior-New York, the salon is the first of its kind and is decorated by Nicolas de Gunsbourg.
Creation of Christian Dior Perfumes – New York.

1949. Launch of a new perfume called 'Diorama'.
In marketing Dior stockings in the United States, the firm introduces the licensing system there.

1950. Ties made and sold under licence, followed by all other accessories. Within three years this system has been taken up by all the other fashion houses.

1951. Christian Dior Furs opens in Paris.
Agreement between *Holt Renfrew* and Christian Dior-New York covering the whole of Canada and granting exclusive reproduction rights on all collections and accessories made by Dior in New York and Paris. Agreement with *El Encanto* in Havana relating to exclusive reproduction rights on Dior designs in New York and Paris.
Conversion of 'La Colle Noire', Montauroux's house in the Var, involving extensive rebuilding work.

1952. The House of Dior consolidates its position in Europe by setting up a company in London, Christian Dior Models Limited. Agreement signed with the *House of Youth* in Sydney granting exclusive reproduction rights on Dior's New York designs.
Exclusive contract with *Los Gobelinos* in Santiago, Chile, covering Dior's *Haute Couture* designs in Paris.

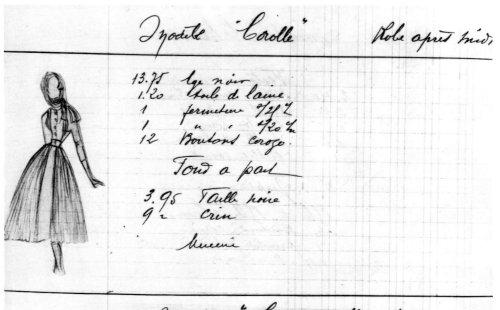

Excerpt from Dior's notebook dealing with the 'Corolle' design.

A New Look model explained by the master with the help of his cane.

Choosing the fabrics – a rite which would seem insane to the uninitiated.

Dior and his earliest ties, seen here with the inspirational figure of Germaine Bricard. *Photo by Maywald.*

Fashion parade at the Sorbonne in the course of a conference on
fashion in 1955.

1953. Opening of a joint boutique with Cartier in Caracas.

Agreement signed with *Palacio de Hiero* in Mexico for exclusive reproduction rights for made-to-measure designs from Dior's *Haute Couture* division in Paris. In January Dior enters into partnership with the shoe designer Roger Vivier. Yves Saint Laurent, then aged seventeen and the winner of a competition organized by the Association of Wool Manufacturers, is noticed by Dior.

1954. Fashion parade for the British royal family at Blenheim Palace. On 29 July Dior launches his 'French Bean' Line or 'Flat Look', thus marking the end of the New Look.

On 3 August he delivers a lecture at the Sorbonne.

1955. At nineteen, Yves Saint Laurent becomes Dior's first and only assistant.

Official opening of the Grande Boutique on the corner of the Avenue Montaigne and the Rue François Ier.

Launch of Dior lipsticks, followed by a whole series of beauty products.

1957. Dior dies of a heart attack on 24 October, during a course of treatment at Montecatini. Yves Saint Laurent, his heir apparent, is called upon to ensure the firm's artistic direction. Jacques Rouët takes over as manager.

1958. On 30 January Yves Saint Laurent launches his first collection under the Dior label, the famous 'Trapeze' Line. Marc Bohan is appointed artistic director of the London subsidiary.

1959. In June, the first presentation at Moscow, in the presence of Yves Saint Laurent.

In 1954 hemlines start to rise again, but without ever revealing the knee, which for Dior was the ugliest part of a woman's body.

Dior's grave in the cemetery at Caillan. *Photo by Maywald.*

1960. Yves Saint Laurent is called up, and leaves Dior, having designed six collections. He is succeeded by Marc Bohan, then aged thirty-four.

1961. Marc Bohan presents his first collection, the 'Slim Look', under the Dior label.

1962. Yves Saint Laurent opens his own fashion house.

1963. Roger Vivier leaves Dior in order to establish himself independently. Launch of the perfume 'Diorling'.

1966. Launch of a perfume for men, 'Eau Sauvage'.

1967. Marc Bohan's assistant, Philippe Guibourgé, creates 'Miss Dior', the first line in ready-to-wear women's clothing in France to bear Dior's name. The 'Baby Dior' Boutique is opened.

Frédéric Castet.

1968. Launch of Christian Dior Knitwear Coordinates. The Dior perfume business is sold to the Moët-Hennessy group. Frédéric Castet takes over as manager of the *Haute Fourrure* division of Christian Dior-Paris.

1970. Creation of the line 'Christian Dior Monsieur'.
A new Dior boutique is opened at Parly Deux, decorated by Gae Aulenti.

1972. Launch of the perfume 'Diorella'.

1973. Creation of a ready-to-wear fur collection in France, later manufactured under licence in the United States, Canada and Japan.

1978. Compulsory liquidation of the Marcel Boussac Group and its assignment to the Agache Group.

1979. Launch of the perfume 'Dioressence'.

1980. Launch of men's perfume 'Jules'.

1984. Bernard Arnault assumes control of the Agache Group, owners of Christian Dior.

1985. Bernard Arnault is appointed chairman and managing director of the House of Dior. Jacques Rouët, having reached retirement age, steps down. Launch of the perfume 'Poison'.

1986. The national and international activities of the House of Dior represent a total turnover of around six thousand million francs.

1987. The Musée de la Mode devotes an exhibition to Dior to mark the thirtieth anniversary of his death.

For his home in Paris he bought beautiful things, and paid a lot
for them. *Photo by Savitry.*

CHRISTIAN DIOR AND THE CINEMA

1942. *Le Lit à colonnes* by Roland Tual.
1942. *Lettres d'amour* by Claude Autant-Lara.
1944. *Echec au roi* by Paulin.
1945. *Sylvie et le fantôme* by Claude Autant-Lara.
1945. *Pamela ou l'énigme du temple* by Pierre de Herain.
1946. *Pour une nuit d'amour* by E. T. Greville.
1947. *Le Silence est d'or* by René Clair.
1947. *La Valse de Paris* by Marcel Achard.
1947. *Jeanne d'Arc* (not made).
1949. *Ce siècle a 50 ans* by Denise Tual; a dress for Geneviève Page.
1950. *Stage Fright* by Alfred Hitchcock; dress for Marlene Dietrich.
1951. *No Highway in the Sky* by Henry Koster; two-piece suit for Marlene Dietrich.
1955. Dresses for Zizi Jeanmaire in *Anything Goes* with Bing Crosby.
1956. *The Ambassador's Daughter* by N. Krasna; a dress for Olivia de Haviland.
1956. *The Little Hut* by Mark Robson; fourteen dresses for Ava Gardner.

Olivia de Haviland in *The Ambassador's Daughter* by Norman Krasna.
1956.

Yvonne Printemps (centre) in Marcel Achard's *La Valse de Paris*.
1947. *Photo by Cinémathèque française.*

Marlene Dietrich in Alfred Hitchcock's *Stage Fright*. 1950.

Yada's dress in Roland Tual's film *Le Lit à colonnes*. 1942.

Madeleine Renaud trying on an evening gown in 1950. *Photo by Maywald.*

Edwige Feuillère trying on an evening gown in 1950.

CHRISTIAN DIOR AND THE THEATRE

1939. *The School for Scandal* by Sheridan, produced by Marcel Herrand at the Théâtre des Mathurins.
Captain Smith by Jean Blanchon at the Théâtre des Mathurins.
1944. *Au petit bonheur* by M. G. Sauvageon at the Théâtre Gramont.
1947. *L'Apollon de Marsac* by Jean Giraudoux at the Théâtre de l'Athénée.
1953. *Pour Lucrèce* by Jean Giraudoux at the Théâtre Marigny.

CHRISTIAN DIOR AND THE BALLET

1947. *Treize danses* by Roland Petit at the Théâtre des Champs-Elysées.

Madeleine Renaud and Simone Valère in Giraudoux's *Pour Lucrèce*.
1953. *Photo by André Ostier.*

The costumes for Sheridan's *School for Scandal* at the Théâtre des Mathurins, designed by Dior in 1939 before he had made a name for himself.

Odette Joyeux's costume in Claude Autant-Lara's 1942 film *Lettres d'amour*. Photo by *Cinémathèque française*.

Odette Joyeux in Claude Autant-Lara's *Lettres d'amour*.

Dior in his garden at the Moulin du Coudret in Milly. He believed in the language of cards. *Photo by Louise Dahl-Wolfe.*

ACKNOWLEDGMENTS

The publisher wishes to thank Françoise Giroud and Sacha Van Dorssen for their collaboration on the present volume as author and photographer respectively.

He would also like to thank the following for their invaluable assistance: Monsieur Bernard Arnault, Monsieur Marc Bohan, Monsieur Frédéric Castet, Madame Catherine Dior, Madame Elisabeth Flory, Madame Nadine Gasc, Monsieur Dominique Morlotti, Mademoiselle Florence Muller, Monsieur Jacques Rouët, Madame Alexandra Tchernoff El Khoury, Princess Marie-Christine Wittgenstein and Monsieur Nicolas Clive-Worms, all of whom have placed their personal reminiscences and archives at his disposal.

He wishes to express his gratitude to all those people who have helped him in his research and enabled him to produce this book.

A.G.I.P. agency, Monsieur Paul Audrain, Monsieur Jean-Nicolas Aurange, Monsieur Richard Avedon, Madame Lilian Bassman, Mademoiselle Véronique Belloir, Beck of the Femme agency, Madame Alfred Bloomingdale, Maître Blum, Monsieur Edouard Boizel, Monsieur Philippe Boizel, Mademoiselle Bonamy of the Department of Prints at the Bibliothèque Nationale, Madame Françoise Bornstein, Monsieur Jacques Boulay, Madame Boulat, Monsieur Guy Bourdin, Monsieur Billy Boy, Madame Monique Bromet, Mademoiselle Jenny Capitain, Madame Marguerite Carré, Countess René de Chambrun, Madame Anne de Cizancourt, Monsieur Henry Clarke, Jean-François and Françoise of the Laboratoire Clolus, Madame Coisy – Christian Dior Perfumes, Mademoiselle Nadine Coleno, Madame Elisabeth-Ann Coleman of the Brooklyn Museum, Madame Lydia Cullen of Sotheby's, Bruno at the Laboratoire Daguerre, Madame Louise Dahl-Wolfe, Mademoiselle Paule Delaitre, Madame Josette Demedicis, Madame Shelley Dowell, Mademoiselle Carole Ducass, Madame Diana Edkins – Condé-Nast USA, Charles Faubert for Jacques Dessange, Madame Jackie Fixo for the Scoop agency, Madame Marian François Poncet, Monsieur Roberto Frankenberg, Monsieur Stanley Garfinkel, Monsieur Guillaume Garnier, Musée de la Mode et du Costume – Palais Galliéra, Monsieur Christopher Green, Monsieur Didier Grumbach, Madame Mimi Guevara Herrera de Uslar, Monsieur Hatami, Madame Olivia de Haviland, Mademoiselle Maris Hellen, Madame Aimée de Herren, Monsieur Horst, Monsieur Andrew P. Isherwood, Société Charles Jourdan, Monsieur Jérôme Jullien-Cornic, Mademoiselle Lydia Kamitzis, Monsieur Robert Kaufman, Madame Betty Klarnett – *Harper's Bazaar*, Monsieur Langberg – Christian Dior London, Madame Le Goubun, Madame Astrid Lehaire, Monsieur Eric Le Tourneur d'Ison, Louise at the City agency, Madame Gina Lollobrigida, Madame Pat Mac Cabe, Madame Meriel Mac Cooey – *Sunday Times Magazine*, Madame Frances Laughlin-Gill, Madame Charlette Maderni, Countess de Malleray de Barre, Monsieur and Madame Marquis, Madame R. Massigli, Monsieur Anthony Mazzola, Madame Alice Morgaine – *Jardin des Modes*, Madame Martine Mollard, Monsieur Dominique Morlotti, Madame Ute Mundt – Condé-Nast France, Monsieur Patrick Neiertz, Madame Jutta Nieman, Monsieur Helmut Newton, Madame Ilka Nolasco, Baroness Ordioni, Monsieur Ostier, Monsieur Norman Parkinson, Monsieur Irving Penn, Madame Johanne Pierce – Christian Dior New York, Madame Brigitte Poignet, Monsieur Jean Poniatowski, Monsieur Philippe Pottier, Monsieur Yves Prigent, H.R.H. Princess Caroline of Monaco, H.R.H. Prince Rainier III, Madame Regi Relang, Madame Madeleine Renaud, Monsieur Willy Ronis, Rosaline of the Sky agency, Madame Danielle Roux, Monsieur Henri Sauguet, Monsieur Seeberger, Madame Simone Simon, Sipa Press agency, Sigma agency, Monsieur Irving Solero – Fashion Institute of Technology, Madame Alice Springs, Galerie Stanley Wise, Monsieur Rick Tardif, Monsieur Jean-Michel Tardy, Madame Jeannie Tourniaire, Madame Susan Train, Madame Denise Tual, Madame Sylvie Vartan, Violetta, Madame Francine Vormese, Madame Alec Weisweiller, Madame Oscar Wyatt, Monsieur Eric Wright, Madame Raymonde Zehnaker, and the Atelier Michel Boudin, Atelier Elisabeth Gallet, Atelier Claude Laurent, Atelier Andrée Renaud, Atelier Amparo Sorribes.

LIST OF LENDERS

The publisher is grateful to the following for the loan of individual articles: Monsieur Bechara El Khoury for his mother's dress (192), Madame A. Bloomingdale (281), Countess R. de Chambrun (138), Madame Mimi Guevara de Herrera Uslar (230), Countess de Malleray de Barre (274), Madame R. Massigli (106), H.R.H. Prince Rainier III (238, 239), H.R.H. Princess Caroline of Monaco (245, 292), Madame Danielle Roux (179, 201, 258), Madame Simone Simon (144, 145), Jeannie Tourniaire (193, 224), Madame Alec Weisweiller (132, 133 [autumn/winter 1955], 223, 231, 249, 251, 255 [autumn/winter 1957], 261), Madame Oscar Wyatt (282), and the *Musée Christian Dior* (89, 92-3 [gift of Madame Nolasco], 107, 128 [gift of Baroness Ordioni], 129, 200 [gift of Madame Bricard], 220, 245, 246, 247, 250, 278), the *Musée de la Mode et du Costume,* Palais Galliéra (135 [hat veil donated by Lady Deterding], 148, 149, 200 [hat donated by André Buffet]), *Private Collection of Billy Boy* (132-3 [brooch], 135 [brooch signed by Christian Dior], 146-7 [maker's label designed by Roger Vivier], 148, 175, 189 [Christian Dior jewelry by Mitchell Maer], 192 [Christian Dior jewelry by Mitchell Maer], 193 (jewelry by Mitchell Maer], 200 [gloves], 209 [Christian Dior label designed by Roger Vivier], 223 [Christian Dior bracelet and brooch by Mitchell Maer], 231 [Christian Dior jewelry by Mitchell Maer], 254 [shoe label designed by Roger Vivier]), *Collection du Département des Textiles de l'U.C.A.D.* (216, 234, 235, 252, 253 [embroidery by Rébé]), *Collection U.F.A.C.* (94-5 [donated by Madame Brodie], 159 [donated by Madame Malitte Matta], 182, 183, 196-7 [donated by Madame Kaindl], 204, 210-11 [donated by Madame Arturo Lopez Willshaw], 213 [donated by Madame Brodie], 214-15 [donated by Madame de Bord], 221, 227 [donated by Madame Michèle Rosier], 241, 259 [donated by Madame Alice Chavanne de Dalmassy], 266 [donated by Countess Latour de Geay], 267 [donated by Madame de Bord]), *Condé-Nast U.S.A.* (112, 113, 265, 266), *Fashion Institute of Technology* (90, 91, 136, 170), *Harper's Bazaar* (90, 91, 136), and *Sotheby's of London* (22, 141).

The cover of *Time* magazine. Dior's word was law.

7/03   41   5/02
3/06   45   5/05
7/11   58   3/11
  9/10 (67) 4/10